# JESUS
# OVER
# EVERY
# THING

## UNCOMPLICATING THE DAILY STRUGGLE TO PUT JESUS FIRST

### STUDY GUIDE + STREAMING VIDEO
### SIX SESSIONS

# LISA WHITTLE

HarperChristian Resources

*Jesus Over Everything Study Guide*
© 2020, 2024 by Lisa Whittle

Published in Grand Rapids, Michigan, by HarperChristian Resources. HarperChristian Resources is a registered trademark of HarperCollins Christian Publishing, Inc.

Requests for information should be addressed to customercare@harpercollins.com.

ISBN 978-0-310-14677-3 (softcover)
ISBN 978-0-310-14678-0 (ebook)

HarperChristian Resources titles may be purchased in bulk for church, business, fundraising, or ministry use. For information, please e-mail ResourceSpecialist@ChurchSource.com.

Published in association with Yates & Yates, LLP, www.yates2.com.

First Printing January 2020 / Printed in the United States of America
24 25 26 27 28  LBC  5 4 3 2 1

# CONTENTS

# INTRODUCTION

# LET ME UNCOMPLICATE THIS FOR YOU

Do you ever struggle to put Jesus first? Do you ever feel like your life is over-complicated? For years, I've been listening to women who say they want to put Jesus first, but they're not sure what that looks like in their everyday life. These same women also readily admit their lives have become over-complicated and they're not sure how to uncomplicate them.

If you can say, "Yes and Amen!" to this, then I'm guessing the reason your life has gotten so complicated is because you have a mixed-up priority order. Believe me, friend, I've been there myself and didn't at first make the connection. That's why I want to help you uncomplicate your life. Not because you need to clean out your closets or throw your calendar out the window, but because we all—me included—keep operating with our mixed-up priority order, while at the same time asking Jesus to help us and bless us.

I'm a bottom-line person and here's the bottom line of this *Jesus Over Everything* study guide experience: Your life will be less complicated if you put Jesus first. Period. That's why we're going to face our "deadly overs" head-on: *over-doing, over-apologizing, over-explaining, over-indulging,* and *over-working.* Because these are some of the actions that lead to over-complicating our lives.

We're also going to look at the Jesus-first life and the better things it offers. After we see the choice, clearly, we will dive into four sessions that take us through the uncomplicating process (with lots of Bible teaching and practical application), and a last wrap-up session to give us final tools to equip and motivate us for the

Jesus-over-everything journey ahead. I have truly poured my heart into this study. To teach this timely word in a season when many of us feel the burden of personal unrest is a powerful gift that I believe will be a game changer.

If you're reading along in *Jesus Over Everything*, you will notice that the eight choice statements in the book—*real over pretty, love over judgment, holiness over freedom, service over spotlight, steady over hype, wisdom over knowledge, honesty over hiding, commitment over mood*—are broken down practically in each chapter to encourage new daily lifestyle choices. We'll use our time together during each study session to talk about how we learn to see the "Jesus over everything" decision each and every day, and how the Jesus over everything life is well within our reach with the help of the Holy Spirit. Jesus wouldn't have told us to put him first if he wasn't willing to help us with the execution of it in our daily life. In every way, he is the God who helps us. The good news I want you to hear right now and in each session is this: you can *absolutely* live this kind of life.

My hope is that *Jesus Over Everything* will have a deep and lasting impact for years because I'm living proof that the right priority order can change *everything* about our lives.

*Lisa Whittle*

# HOW TO USE THIS GUIDE

The *Jesus Over Everything* video study is designed to be experienced in a group setting such as a Bible study, Sunday school class, or any small group gathering. Each session begins with a welcome section, several questions to get you thinking about the topic, and a reading from the Bible. You will then watch a teaching video and engage in some small-group discussion. You will close each session with a time of personal reflection and prayer as a group.

Each person in the group should have her own study guide. Each study guide comes with individual streaming video access (instructions found on the inside front cover) to watch videos from the convenience of your chosen devices at any time—for missed group meetings, for rewatching, for sharing teaching with others, or watching videos individually and then meeting if your group is short on meeting time and that makes the group experience doable and more realistic. We have worked very hard to make gathering around the Word of God and studying accessible and simple.

Multiple translations will be used throughout the study, so whatever translation you have is fine. You are also encouraged to have a copy of the *Jesus Over Everything* book, as reading the book alongside the study will provide you with deeper insights and make the journey more meaningful. (See the "For Next Week" section at the end of each between-studies section for the chapters in the book that correspond to material you and your group are discussing.)

To get the most out of your group experience, keep the following points in mind. First, the real growth in this study will happen during your small-group time. This is where you will process the content of the teaching for the week, ask questions, and learn from others as you hear what God is doing in their lives. For this reason, it is important for you to be fully committed to the group and attend each session so you can build trust and rapport with the other members. If you choose to only go through the motions, or if you refrain from participating, there is a lesser chance you will find what you're looking for during this study.

Second, remember the goal of your small group is to serve as a place where people can share, learn about God, and build intimacy and friendship. For this reason, seek to make your group a safe place. This means being honest about your thoughts and feelings, and listening carefully to everyone else's opinion. (If you are a group leader, there are additional instructions and resources in the back of the book for leading a productive discussion group.)

Third, resist the temptation to fix a problem someone might be having or to correct her theology. Keep everything shared in your group confidential. This will foster a sense of community in your group and create a place where people can be challenged and grow spiritually.

Following your group time, there is personal study material to complete before you meet again. For each session, you may wish to complete the personal study all in one sitting or spread it out over a few days. If you are unable to finish (or even start!) your between-sessions personal study, you should still attend the group study video session. You are still wanted and welcome at the group even if you don't have your "homework" done.

# PUTTING GOD FIRST

HE IS BEFORE ALL THINGS, AND IN
HIM ALL THINGS HOLD TOGETHER.

COLOSSIANS 1:17 NIV

# WELCOME

*Leader, read aloud to the group.*

Today we're talking about something beautiful and powerful: what it means to live a Jesus over everything kind of life. We'll explore the mindsets that often keep us from it and the complications we get into when we try to manage life on our own. We'll see through Scripture how a Jesus-first life is within our reach with the help of the Holy Spirit and encouragement from the Word. Remember: Jesus is willing to help us live this kind of life. It's not something we have to figure out all on our own. So, take a deep breath and let's get started with session one.

And just a helpful heads-up as we get started, this study guide experience isn't going to be about a long list of things to do, or a ton of hardcore spiritual excavation. It's going to be a journey to help you see the truth about what is complicating your life and how to uncomplicate it by putting Jesus first.

# SHARE

*If you or any of your group members are just getting to know one another, take a few minutes to introduce yourselves. Then, to kick things off, briefly discuss one of the following statements:*

Share *one* word you would use to describe your life right now.

— or —

Name *one* area of your life you wish felt less chaotic.

# READ

*Invite someone to read aloud the following passage as "heart prep" for Lisa's teaching. Listen for fresh insights as you hear the verses being read, and then briefly discuss the questions that follow.*

## THE HEALING AT THE POOL

Some time later, Jesus went up to Jerusalem for one of the Jewish festivals. Now there is in Jerusalem near the Sheep Gate a pool, which in Aramaic is called Bethesda and which is surrounded by five covered colonnades. Here a great number of disabled people used to lie—the blind, the lame, the paralyzed. One who was there had been an invalid for thirty-eight years. When Jesus saw him lying there and learned that he had been in this condition for a long time, he asked him, "Do you want to get well?" "Sir," the invalid replied, "I have no one to help me into the pool when the water is stirred. While I am trying to get in, someone else goes down ahead of me." Then Jesus said to him, "Get up! Pick up your mat and walk." At once the man was cured; he picked up his mat and walked. The day on which this took place was a Sabbath, and so the Jewish leaders said to the man who had been healed, "It is the Sabbath; the law forbids you to carry your mat." But he replied, "The man who made me well said to me, 'Pick up your mat and walk.' " So they asked him, "Who is this fellow who told you to pick it up and walk?" The man who was healed had no idea who it was, for Jesus had slipped away into the crowd that was there. Later Jesus found him at the temple and said to him, "See, you are well again. Stop sinning or something worse may happen to you." The man went away and told the Jewish leaders that it was Jesus who had made him well. (John 5:1–15 NIV)

**What is one key insight that stands out to you from this passage?**

Why do you think Jesus asks the man, *"Do you want to get well?"*

Consider as you listen to Lisa's teaching, where you want freedom from complication and chaos in your life?

# WATCH

*Play the video segment for session one. As you watch, use the following outline to record any thoughts or concepts that stand out to you.*

## NOTES
**A simpler life**

> "THINGS IN OUR LIFE GET COMPLICATED OFTEN BEFORE WE KNOW IT. MOST OF US DON'T WILLFULLY CHOOSE IT; WE SILENTLY SLIDE INTO IT."

**The cycle of complication**

**1.** We deflect

> "EVERY TIME WE DEFLECT FROM THINGS WE NEED TO DEAL WITH, WE WITHHOLD OUR OWN HEALING."

John 5: The Man at the Pool of Bethesda—*"Do you want to get well?"*

**2.** We overcompensate for a life we can't control

The deadly overs

> "WE ARE UNDER A FALSE ASSUMPTION THAT THIS OVERDOING IS IN SOME WAY PRODUCING THE HUMILITY AND SELFLESSNESS WE CAN'T SEEM TO OTHERWISE FIND."

**3.** We loathe our life and want to get a new one

> "MOST OF US DON'T NEED A BRAND-NEW LIFE. WE JUST NEED GOD TO RUN OURS."

**How to get things on the right track**

**1.** Jesus is *for* us

**2.** Jesus being *first* is the only way our lives will work

Colossians 1:15–23

The "preeminence" of Christ is just a fancy way to say *"first place"* or *"first."*

*Do I truly believe_____?*

### The Lisa Whittle paraphrase of Colossians 1
- Look at all Jesus has done for you (verses 1–14).
- Remember who Jesus is (verses 15–22).
- And now, make him number one (verse 23).

### The Jesus-over-everything lifestyle
Romans 5:5

Psalm 91:1

> "PUTTING JESUS FIRST IS A CHOICE TO SIMPLIFY OUR LIVES AND HAND OURSELVES BACK OUR OWN SANITY."

John 1:1

### Life is Jesus. Jesus is life.
*"The key to a beautiful life is not self-management; it is to put Jesus first over everything, where he belongs."*

# DISCUSS

*Take a few minutes with your group members to discuss what you just watched and explore these concepts in Scripture.*

**1.** Name one thing that makes your life feel complicated right now:

**2.** According to Lisa, there are several ways we respond to the idea or concept of putting Jesus over everything in our lives. Which of the following do you resonate with the most and why? Share with the group.

☐ I feel overwhelmed at the thought of putting Jesus first.

☐ I feel guilty for not having put him first, before.

☐ I long to have a less complicated life.

☐ I long to live a life where Jesus is in charge and I'm good with it.

☐ Jesus over everything sounds awesome, but I have no idea really how to do it.

**3.** Let's talk about the Cycle of Complication. In what areas of life do you *deflect* the most from things you need to deal with? Share one or two examples with the group. Discuss why deflection seems a better or more convenient solution to complication and yet often causes more complication. Would things change if you confronted and dealt with one of the areas you most deflect from?

**4.** How do we *overcompensate* for a life we can't control (i.e., *over-do, over-apologize, over-book, over-think, over-analyze, over-indulge*)? Discuss how this behavior keeps us from putting Jesus over anything. Discuss the irony and come up with 1–2 ways you can change your over-behaviors to allow Jesus' example and teaching to lead your reactions and responses.

**5.** Share your current priority list, honestly (rank 1–5). Does it feel like your priorities are working for you or against you? If you were to put God as a priority, describe how you think things would be different.

**6.** Share one word that would describe what it would feel like if you didn't have to over-manage your life anymore.

# PRAY

*Pray as a group before you close your time together. Use this space to keep track of prayer requests and group updates.*

# BETWEEN-SESSIONS PERSONAL STUDY

This week, start your *Jesus Over Everything* personal study by spending some time with God each day. Reflect on the material you covered during your group time by engaging in any or all of the following between-sessions exercises. At the start of the next session you will have a few minutes to share any insights you learned. But remember, the primary goal of these between-sessions exercises is for your own spiritual growth, not so you have the perfect answer for group discussion. And if you haven't done so already, let me encourage you to read chapter one of *Jesus Over Everything*.

## WEEKLY REFLECTION: SESSION ONE

*Before you begin the between-sessions exercises, briefly review your video notes for session one. In the space below, write down the most significant point you took away from this session's teaching.*

Reflect on the word you chose at the end of the group session—the word that comes to mind when you think about not having to over-manage your life anymore. List 2–3 *specific* ways that word will influence your decisions and actions this week as you work toward putting Jesus over everything else.

## DAY ONE: SHIFT YOUR FOCUS

In order to live the uncomplicated *Jesus Over Everything* life, we have to shift our focus from "ourselves first" to "Jesus foremost." It's that simple; yet, it's something we don't often do. But we can't make this shift until we identify what we're currently focused on.

First, let me explain what I mean by the word *focus* just so we're all on the same page. When I talk about *focus*, I mean whatever it is that consumes us the most—our time, our attention, our thoughts, our actions, our words, our finances. Our focus is often what keeps us up at night, and what keeps us occupied throughout the day. Too much focus on anyone or anything but Jesus is what makes life more complicated than it needs to be. And if we try to uncomplicate our lives without the help of Jesus, we stay in the cycle of what I call the *deadly overs*, where we overdo it in key areas of our lives. So, first up: we've got to do a little digging out of the *deadly overs* in order to have an honest assessment of where our focus lies and where it needs to shift to Jesus.

Consider how the *deadly overs* complicate your life and consume your focus using the chart below. Fill in the blank boxes at the bottom with your own *deadly overs*. TAKE YOUR TIME going through this. It will likely take a few attempts to uncover your *deadly overs*.

## SELF-ASSESSMENT: *THE DEADLY OVERS*

| MY DEADLY-OVERS | Real-life examples | What complication is this causing me? |
|---|---|---|
| over-doing | | |
| over-apologizing | | |
| over-explaining | | |
| over-analyzing | | |
| over-indulging | | |
| | | |
| | | |
| | | |

Now, using the chart below, consider how the *Jesus overs* uncomplicate your life and help shift your focus. Fill in the blank boxes at the bottom with your own *Jesus overs*.

## JESUS ASSESSMENT: *THE JESUS OVERS*

| THE JESUS OVERS | Real-life examples | How would this uncomplicate my life? |
|---|---|---|
| Jesus over my prayer life | | |
| Jesus over my thoughts | | |
| Jesus over my words | | |
| Jesus over how I spend my time | | |
| Jesus over my relationships | | |
| Jesus over my sex life | | |
| | | |
| | | |
| | | |

Read Philippians 4:4–9. List the seven attributes—or areas of focus—of the **Jesus-over-everything** kind of life mentioned by the apostle Paul in verse 8.

# COMMENTARY ON PHILIPPIANS 4:6–9

God needs not to be told our wants or desires; he knows them better than we do; but he will have us show that we value the mercy, and feel our dependence on him. The peace of God, the comfortable sense of being reconciled to God, and having a part in his favor, and the hope of the heavenly blessedness, are a greater good than can be fully expressed. This peace will keep our hearts and minds through Christ Jesus; it will keep us from sinning under troubles, and from sinking under them; keep us calm and with inward satisfaction. Believers are to get and to keep a good name; a name for good things with God and good men. We should walk in all the ways of virtue, and abide therein; then, whether our praise is of men or not, it will be of God. The apostle is for an example. His doctrine and life agreed together. The way to have the God of peace with us, is to keep close to our duty. All our privileges and salvation arise in the free mercy of God; yet the enjoyment of them depends on our sincere and holy conduct. These are works of God, pertaining to God, and to him only are they to be ascribed, and to no other, neither men, words, nor deeds.

–from *Matthew Henry's Concise Commentary on the Whole Bible*

- **Read:** Reread Philippians 4:4–6 and think deeply on the passage.
- **Look up:** Find the word *peace* in a concordance and explore other passages where this word also appears.
- **Explore:** Consider just how thorough and true this peace is that God is defining for us when we put Jesus over everything.

**Take Action:** Remember my "shopping fast" story? Yep, you know where this is headed. Consider fasting—or taking a break—from something this week that consumes your focus and contributes to a *deadly over* in your life. It can be shopping, or a few extra activities, or swapping out some Scripture meditation and breath work for the overthinking or overanalyzing you do on a regular basis. Or ask the Lord to help you be aware of over-apology and for a week work on saying only necessary, honest ones . . . or stop explaining yourself every time you feel misunderstood. The idea is to pick something that usually keeps you in an unhealthy cycle and commit to detox from it with God's help this week.

THIS WEEK I WILL FAST FROM:

_____

**Pray:** Take a few moments to reflect on your answers to the questions and invite God into the ways you want to uncomplicate your life.

## DAY TWO: THE TWO-DEGREE DIFFERENCE

Often, when we think about the things we want to change in our lives, our impulse is to make big, drastic changes. We get an "all or nothing" mindset and think a 180-degree turn is what's required, when most of the time it only takes a two-degree difference to set our lives on a different trajectory of choices. Just two degrees can be powerful and life-altering. The phrase, "two-degree difference," is often used in science and psychology to describe slight changes that steer us in a new direction out of the course of catastrophe. For example, today we live nine-degrees away from the last ice age where no human life was viable. A slight two degrees in temperature moves us closer or further from a *significant* change in our climate.

While I don't want to be overly dramatic about this concept, I think it's helpful to be mindful of the fact that just because your life isn't working now doesn't mean you need to get a whole different life. Sometimes you just need to make a few small adjustments—the two-degree difference. My guess is most of us innately know when things are not working for us, but sometimes we just don't know how to change . . . or we're afraid of that change. As you answer the questions below, consider how a few small adjustments in your life could have great and significant impact on the change you desire and the life you long to live.

1.  Briefly review your reflections from the last between-sessions exercise on the *deadly overs*. Which deadly over causes the most amount of pain, complication, or chaos for you?

2.  When was the last time life seemed uncomplicated for you? List a few major markers of that time period that stand out as differences from how you are experiencing life today.

3.  **Read Romans 5:1–5.** Not only do we have Jesus as the example of the way to live our lives, but we also have the Holy Spirit as our guide. How does this influence your perspective on the changes you need to make right now? Think about a specific way you can engage the Holy Spirit on a daily basis to alter one aspect of chaos or discord or complication in your life right now. Write a declaration statement to claim your commitment to letting the Holy Spirit take over whatever is most in need.

I WILL GIVE

_____

TO THE HOLY SPIRIT AND TRUST HIS GUIDANCE.

4.  How have you made matters worse by trying to do it all on your own? **Read Romans 8:26–27.** Consider where the Holy Spirit may be interceding on your behalf already. Describe specific circumstances where letting him lead you would uncomplicate your life right now.

UNDERSTANDING YOUR BIBLE

# COMMENTARY ON ROMANS 5

This passage implies that we are at peace with God already (v. 1). With peace established, we now have access to God's presence. The wall of partition (or separation) has been removed. This peace is not a guarded truce subject to new warfare. It is a permanent peace. And the New Testament hope (v. 2) is the assurance of something not yet fully experienced, and quite different from uncertain, wishful thinking. That this hope will not be frustrated is guaranteed here and now by the love of God that the Holy Spirit pours into believers' hearts (vv. 4, 5).

–paraphrased from *New Geneva Study Bible*

- **Read:** Reread Romans 5:1–5 and think deeply on the passage.
- **Look up:** Find the words *Holy Spirit* in a concordance and explore other passages where the Holy Spirit appears as a guide.
- **Explore:** Now that we have access to God's presence through the Holy Spirit, consider what it means for you to have permanent peace and unwavering hope in Jesus.

**5.** **Read Psalm 91.** I'm a big believer in the idea that the best way to make change in our lives is to first find our strength and refuge in God. How does finding strength and refuge in God help to uncomplicate your life?

6. Do you find it difficult to connect your good and the glory of Jesus on a daily basis? If so, consider why and make note of it. If not, describe how you view your good as connected to Jesus' glory and what drives that perspective for you.

**Take Action:** I want you to seriously consider the changes you need to make in your life. Not just the big changes, but the small changes too—those changes that make a two-degree difference for you. And then I want you to start practicing a few of them this week. The point is not to feel more overwhelmed than you already do, or make life more complicated than it already seems. The point is to help you take baby steps toward uncomplicating your life as you learn to trust Jesus with the details of your life.

THE TWO-DEGREE DIFFERENCE I WANT TO MAKE THIS WEEK IS:

_____

**Pray:** Take a few moments to reflect on your answers to the questions and your action step for this week as you invite God into the changes you want to make.

## DAY THREE: FINDING HOPE IN JESUS FIRST

If you're reading along in the book, you find out in a story I tell that I do *not* do well with second place. I could tell you more about this, but what I'd rather talk about is how even those of us who might not consider ourselves competitive in nature struggle to be in the passenger seat of our lives.

Have you ever noticed how we tend to wait until things get complicated or chaotic before we reach out and ask God for help? Most of us beg God for help in the middle of a life with mixed-up priorities, and yet when we're finally willing to surrender and put God over all things, the complications seem to lessen and our lives are filled with hope. If only we could learn to do this on first-impulse every time our life gets complicated. And here's the secret of this session: *I think we can.* Remember the *Lisa Whittle paraphrase* of Colossians 1:15–23 from our teaching session? Just in case you don't, here it is: *Look at all Jesus has done for you; remember who Jesus is; now make him number one.* The more we soak in this truth, the faster it seeps out in our behavior when our life gets out of control.

I've far from perfected *anything* (waiting on heaven for that), but after years of giving my own capabilities a whirl, learning the hard way, and then finally learning how to defer to Jesus, I'm living proof that over time, putting Jesus first can in some ways become surprisingly automatic. (And in other ways, you will fight for it, every day.) If you choose to put Jesus in first place, he will bless you with contentment and peace to replace the confliction and fill your life with hope. He will sort out the things you need to sort out and he will do a perfect job managing your imperfect life. Consider how you can put Jesus first in your life as you answer these questions:

1. What happens when we put ourselves first in our lives over and over again?

2. **Read Matthew 22:34–40.** How does Jesus uncomplicate the gospel message for the religious leaders and disciples with the *Greatest Commandment*? Rewrite the breakdown below.

3. According to this passage, how would your life be less complicated if you followed Jesus' command? Take a serious look at whether or not your daily experience reflects the two behaviors Jesus claims as the greatest priority for your life. What changes if you change your priorities?

---

UNDERSTANDING YOUR BIBLE

# WHAT DOES THE WORD
# *COMMANDMENT* MEAN?

In the original Greek, *commandment* means: An ordinance, injunction, command, law. I.e., an authoritative prescription.

ἐντολὴ / entolē

This word appears 67 times throughout the New Testament. It refers to commandment(s), instructions, orders, requirements.

–from Strong's 1785 and *NAS Exhaustive Concordance*

- **Read:** Also read Mark 12:28–34 and Deuteronomy 6:4–5.
- **Look up:** This original commandment from Deuteronomy 6 is considered the *Shema*. Do a little research on the *Shema* to see why and how often it was practiced in ancient Israel.
- **Explore:** Consider what it means for you to love God with all of your *heart, soul, mind, and strength*.

---

**4.** Which areas of your life are most noticeably different when you take Jesus' command literally? Think about your emotional, physical, and active states of being.

Emotional:

Physical:

Active:

**5.** **Read John 1:1–14.** According to this passage, how does Jesus simplify the gospel message for all and uncomplicate our relationship with God?

**6.** Putting Jesus first gives us hope that our lives can actually be uncomplicated and simple. Name 1–3 particular area(s) of your life that need the hope of Jesus today.

**Take Action:** Putting Jesus first sounds like the "right" thing to say, but the hard thing to do. But here's a little encouragement for you. Life is about our choices. And we're already making choices every single day. You just may need to make some different ones. There's no better time to start making different choices to put Jesus first in your life than right now. So, let's get started.

I WILL CHOOSE TO PUT JESUS FIRST THIS WEEK BY:

_____

**Pray:** Take a few moments to reflect on your answers to the questions and your action step by inviting God into your desire to put Jesus first over everything in your life.

# GOING DEEPER (IF YOU WANT MORE)

**Read Joshua 24.** Up until this point in history, the Israelites were a promise-breaking group of people. And in this passage, we hear Joshua pleading with them to make a change—to take their spiritual lives in a new direction. Joshua recaps God's goodness toward the Israelites and reminds them that the only way their lives would work from this point forward was to place their trust in God. My translation of this passage as it relates to our lives today: *Put Jesus first.*

Spend extra time in prayer today as you consider how Joshua's message to the Israelites relates to your life and your situation today. Perhaps you need to be reminded of God's goodness and remember the only way forward is to place your trust in God by putting Jesus first.

**Use this space to jot down notes or thoughts as they come to mind.**

**For Next Week:** Review chapter one in *Jesus Over Everything* and use the space below to write any insights or questions from your personal study that you want to discuss at the next group meeting. The teaching for session two comes from chapters two and seven in *Jesus Over Everything.*

# BEING REAL

THEN YOU WILL KNOW THE TRUTH,
AND THE TRUTH WILL SET YOU FREE.

JOHN 8:32 NIV

# WELCOME

*Leader, read aloud to the group.*

Today we're talking about something so simple, and yet, so very important: *being real.* And we're tackling two choices most crucial to being real: choosing *real over pretty* and *honesty over hiding.* These two go hand in hand because you can't be real without being honest. Choosing to hide parts of ourselves by not being real is actually the choice to manage and control our lives instead of trusting God to do so. When we do this, we're on a constant quest for other people's approval, thinking their approval will simplify our lives when in reality it only complicates things.

It's like we're managing our own personal PR campaign so that the prettiest and most likeable version of ourselves is what others get from us every waking moment. The truth is, that's just plain *exhausting.* Not only is it exhausting, it's contrary to the life God created us to live, and it affects how we live out the good news of Jesus in the world around us. If we're always seeking pretty instead of real, and if we go on hiding from the truth in our lives, we lose focus on what it means to put Jesus first and we lose our conviction to share the gospel message. *Being real is a gift.* It's a gift we give to ourselves and a gift we give to others. When we choose to be real, it inspires others to be real too.

The hope for us moving forward with this Jesus-over-everything journey is that we will see the truth about what is complicating our lives and learn how to uncomplicate them by putting Jesus first. So let's start today by *being real.*

# SHARE

*Briefly discuss one of the following statements:*

- Share one of your take action exercises from your between-sessions exercises. How has this made a difference for you as you put Jesus first?

— or —

- Name *one* area of your life you wish felt more real and less like a facade.

# READ

*Invite someone to read aloud the following passage as "heart prep" for Lisa's teaching. Listen for fresh insights as you hear the verses being read, and then briefly discuss the questions that follow.*

## JESUS TALKS WITH A SAMARITAN WOMAN

Now Jesus learned that the Pharisees had heard that he was gaining and baptizing more disciples than John— although in fact it was not Jesus who baptized, but his disciples. So he left Judea and went back once more to Galilee. Now he had to go through Samaria. So he came to a town in Samaria called Sychar, near the plot of ground Jacob had given to his son Joseph. Jacob's well was there, and Jesus, tired as he was from the journey, sat down by the well. It was about noon. When a Samaritan woman came to draw water, Jesus said to her, "Will you give me a drink?" (His disciples had gone into the town to buy food.) The Samaritan woman said to him, "You are a Jew and I am a Samaritan woman. How can you ask me for a drink?" (For Jews do not associate with Samaritans.) Jesus answered her, "If you knew the gift of God and who it is that asks you for a drink, you would have asked him and he would have given you living water." "Sir," the woman said, "you have nothing to draw with and the well is deep. Where can you get this living water? Are you greater than our father Jacob, who gave us the well and drank from it himself, as did also his sons and his livestock?" Jesus answered, "Everyone who drinks this water will be thirsty again, but whoever drinks the water I give them will never thirst. Indeed, the water I give them will become in them a spring of water welling up to eternal life." The woman said to him, "Sir, give me this water so that I won't get thirsty and have to keep coming here to draw water." He told her, "Go, call your husband and come back." "I have no husband," she replied.

Jesus said to her, "You are right when you say you have no husband. The fact is, you have had five husbands, and the man you now have is not your husband. What you have just said is quite true." "Sir," the woman said, "I can see that you are a prophet. Our ancestors worshiped on this mountain, but you Jews claim that the place where we must worship is in Jerusalem." "Woman," Jesus replied, "believe me, a time is coming when you will worship the Father neither on this mountain nor in Jerusalem. You Samaritans worship what you do not know; we worship what we do know, for salvation is from the Jews. Yet a time is coming and has now come when the true worshipers will worship the Father in the Spirit and in truth, for they are the kind of worshipers the Father seeks. God is spirit, and his worshipers must worship in the Spirit and in truth." The woman said, "I know that Messiah" (called Christ) "is coming. When he comes, he will explain everything to us." Then Jesus declared, "I, the one speaking to you—I am he." (John 4:1–26 NIV)

**What is one key insight that stands out to you from this passage?**

**Why do you think Jesus said to the Samaritan woman, *"Go, call your husband and come back,"* when he already knew her situation?**

Consider as you listen to Lisa's teaching, where you want freedom from feeling "fake" or from a pattern of dishonesty.

# WATCH

*Play the video segment for session two. As you watch, use the following outline to record any thoughts or concepts that stand out to you.*

## NOTES
**The spiral of social media and Luke Lang**

    Puree.

Ezekiel 11:19

Luke's kind of real

*"Being real is a gift we give to others, and also a gift we give to ourselves."*

**The consequences and complications of not being real**

"IF YOUR GOAL IS TO BE LIKED AND ACCEPTED BY EVERYONE, WELCOME TO A LIFE OF EXHAUSTION."

**Not being real affects how we live out the gospel of Jesus Christ**
The Fight: for people to love me vs. for people to love God

**Uncluttering our lives**

**Jesus-over-everything declaration**

"LIKE ME OR NOT, I JUST PRAY THAT YOU CANNOT DENY THE PRESENCE OF GOD IN MY LIFE."

**Our Jesus-over-everything choices this session**
Real over pretty

Honesty over hiding

"TRUTH, ACCORDING TO THE WORD, SETS US FREE."

Isaiah 53:2

Luke 19—the story of Zacchaeus

"[JESUS] INSPIRES US TO RISE TO THE PEOPLE
HE CREATED US TO BE JUST BY LOVING AND
ACCEPTING US JUST AS WE ARE."

**Real is what we want. Be honest and come clean.**

# DISCUSS

*Take a few minutes with your group members to discuss what you just watched and explore these concepts in Scripture.*

**1.** Name and share one thing that makes your life feel not-so-pretty right now. Now think of one area you feel compelled to come clean about, trusting God to be there as you let go of it. If you feel comfortable, share with the group and experience the freedom in vulnerable honesty before sisters.

**2.** Lisa says, *"Being real is a gift we give to others, and also a gift we give to ourselves."* How has this been true for you? Have you ever felt drawn to the realness of someone in the same way Lisa was drawn to the realness of Luke Lang? What was at the root of the attraction?

**3.** Be honest: do you care more about other people's approval or acceptance than you do about Jesus'? How has that need contributed to exhaustion in your life, and kept you from putting Jesus first?

**4.** Which is more of a struggle for you: being *real over being pretty* or being *honest over hiding?* Name one area in your life where you are consistently tempted to choose pretty over real or hiding over honesty. Discuss why.

**5.** How does loving God and placing Jesus first in your life help you choose to be *real* and *honest*? Name a specific choice you recently made (or need to make) to be *real* and *honest* because of your faith in God. What was the outcome? Was it positive or did your choice meet with conflict or resistance?

**6.** Share one word that would describe what it would feel like if you didn't have to hide or pretend anymore.

# PRAY

*Pray as a group before you close your time together. Use this space to keep track of prayer requests and group updates.*

# BETWEEN-SESSIONS PERSONAL STUDY

This week, start your *Jesus Over Everything* personal study by spending some time with God each day. Reflect on the material you covered during your group time by engaging in any or all of the following between-sessions exercises. Be sure to read the reflection questions before beginning your daily studies and make a few notes in your guide about the experience as you explore what it means to live a Jesus-over-everything kind of life. Remember, the primary goal of these between-sessions exercises is for your own spiritual growth and personal reflection, not so you have the perfect answer for group discussion. And if you haven't done so already, let me encourage you to read chapters two and seven of *Jesus Over Everything*.

## WEEKLY REFLECTION: SESSION TWO

*Briefly review your video notes for session two. In the space below, write down the most significant point you took away from this session.*

Reflect on the word you chose at the end of the group session—the word that comes to mind when you think about not having to hide or pretend anymore. List 2–3 *specific* ways that word will influence your decisions and actions this week as you work toward putting Jesus over everything else.

## DAY ONE: REAL OVER PRETTY

I've said this before, and it bears repeating: In order to live the uncomplicated *Jesus Over Everything* life, we need to shift our focus from ourselves to Jesus. And today we're going to do that by choosing *real over pretty*. First, let me be clear on what I mean by the words *pretty* and *real*. In this context, *pretty* refers to *being consumed by one's perception*. It's the person who cares more about the way others perceive them even at the expense of what's actually true about their lives. *Real* can be defined as humility and truth.

*Here's* why this is so important: because Jesus never tried to be anyone he wasn't. He never tried to fit in or gain popularity. There was nothing pretty about the way he lived or the way he died. There was only humility and truth. And if we truly want to live a *Jesus Over Everything* life, we must get over ourselves and pursue our God-given identity in humility and truth, just as Jesus did.

We were made in the image of God—how's that for real beauty? But we get so wrapped up in the way the world perceives us that we spend so much time lugging around our own set of beauty baggage—what my friend Shari calls our own *beauty wounds*. In order to let go of that baggage and those unhealthy standards, we have to change our definition of what is truly worthy and attractive. We have to exchange our idea of *pretty* for God's explanation of *real,* as we see lived out through the humble life of Jesus. I'm with you, so let's tackle this together.

Consider how choosing *real over pretty* affects your life. Using the chart below, think about real-life examples of when you've chosen to maintain a false perception instead of embracing a life of *humility and truth*. Fill in the blank boxes at the bottom with other areas of your life affected by this choice.

| Areas of my life where I've chosen Pretty or Perception over Being Real | Real-life examples | What complication is this causing me? |
|---|---|---|
| Personal life / Relationships | | |
| Social media posts | | |
| Emotional well-being / Your mental health | | |
| Spiritual life that only you know about | | |
| In your community | | |
| Spiritual life with your faith community | | |
| | | |
| | | |

Jesus redefines what it means for us to be *real* throughout the New Testament. He did this with his words and his deeds. Read the following passages and note the way Jesus calls out or lives out *truth and humility by being real*. Then note a few specific ways that choosing this lifestyle can uncomplicate your life as well.

| Jesus redefines REAL | Real-life examples in the world around you | How would this uncomplicate my life? |
| --- | --- | --- |
| Strength<br>*Hebrews 4:15* | | |
| Self-control<br>*Luke 22:42* | | |
| Humility<br>*Philippians 2:5–8* | | |
| Honesty<br>*Hebrews 5:7–9* | | |
| Leadership<br>*Hebrews 6:19–20* | | |
| Empathy & Kindness<br>*Hebrews 2:14–17* | | |
| Others-centered<br>*1 Peter 2:21–24* | | |

**Read Isaiah 53:2.** According to this passage, there was nothing special about the appearance of Jesus. In fact, Jesus was most likely a small, non-descript young Jewish man. Why do you think this mattered to his ministry or his claim to be the Son of God? How might we have viewed Jesus differently if he had been perceived in a different way? Consider how the truth and humility of Jesus trumps the non-descript perception of Jesus. Also think about the blind spots we have as a society when it comes to the "veneer" of others. How do our perceptions of others—based on the way they look, act, talk, appear—alter the way we see the truth about others?

**Take Action:** Remember my friend who shared openly about her struggles with foster-care parenting? And how I needed to hear her real-life struggles so I would know I wasn't alone just as much as she needed to share them? Similarly, consider one area of life where you could stop pretending you have everything under control, and choose *real over pretty*. It can be parenting, the ways you've messed up as a friend, the doubts and questions you have as a Christ-follower, or the anxiety you're feeling about work in this season. Or ask God to help you be aware of a particular area where you need to stop pretending because someone else needs the gift of your realness in that area of life too. The idea is to pick something that keeps you in an unhealthy cycle of "faking it" and then commit to be real about it with God's help this week.

THIS WEEK I WILL BE REAL ABOUT:

_____

**Pray:** Take a few moments to reflect on your answers to the questions and invite God into the ways you want to uncomplicate your life by being *real*.

# COMMENTARY ON ISAIAH 53:2

The verse seems to take us back to the origin of the Servant's [Jesus's] career, in order to account for the powerful prejudices with which his contemporaries regarded him. From the first he had been mean and unprepossessing in appearance, like a stunted shrub struggling for existence in an arid soil. To this corresponded the first impressions of the people, which were mainly of a negative kind; they found in him nothing that was attractive or desirable.

—from *Cambridge Bible for Schools and Colleges*

- **Read:** Also read Isaiah 52:13–15.
- **Look up:** Consider these two passages from Isaiah 52 and 53 regarding the appearance of Jesus (the *Servant*) by reading them online or from a study Bible. Pay close attention to all the footnotes included in these verses for the full context and meaning.
- **Explore:** Both of these passages mention the appearance of Jesus and then the suffering of Jesus. Consider the connection between the two.

## DAY TWO: HONESTY OVER HIDING

Old habits die hard. I'll be the first person to admit that choosing to emerge from a place of hiding to a place of honesty is no small or easy thing. But here's what I know from my own experience with hiding to coming clean: you will come out of hiding when your desire for healing is greater than your fear of being honest. We often hide until we've had enough of the hiding—the point at which we *hate* whatever we're hiding from or whatever we're feeling enslaved to enough to finally do whatever it takes to free ourselves from its death grip.

But here's the truth: God loves us even though he knows what we're hiding, and he honors our honesty. That's why the Jesus-over-everything lifestyle is a daily practice of honesty with ourselves and others, but most of all, with ourselves and God. Life is not always smooth when you choose honesty over hiding. There will be days when you feel exposed and days when you want to hide again. Expect it and accept it. Freedom is the ultimate prize for a life of honesty. Hiding keeps you from peace, hope, joy and real life. But honesty ushers in the freedom to live the Jesus-over-everything kind of life. So let's get honest together. As you answer the questions below, consider how the truth brings freedom in your life as you choose *honesty over hiding*.

1. Briefly review your reflections from the last between-sessions exercise on *real over pretty*. Consider the ways your choice to pursue pretty or perceptions feeds into the cycle of hiding. As you look over your *pretty over real* chart, what specific things do you hide or hide from the most?

2. How have you been impacted by the dishonesty or hiding of others? And how have others been impacted by your dishonesty or hiding?

3. **Read John 3:19–21.** According to this passage, why do people hide in the darkness? What happens when we stop hiding? Why does Jesus declare the darkness as light to him? How does this fact, that there is nothing kept from God, give you confidence to be more real and honest?

# WHAT DOES THE WORD *DISCIPLE* MEAN?

In the original Greek, *disciple* means: A learner, pupil. From manthano; a learner, i.e., pupil.

(μαθηταί / mathētai)

This word appears 263 times throughout the New Testament. A disciple in the ancient biblical world actively imitated both the life and teaching of the master.

—from Strong's 3101 and Wikipedia

- **Read:** Also read Matthew 4:18–22. Who were the first disciples of Jesus?
- **Look up:** The word *disciple* means something different than our modern idea of a *student*, although these terms are loosely connected. Look up the differences between these two words. Then use your own words to describe the differences.
- **Explore:** Consider what it means for you to be a disciple of Jesus in today's modern world. What actions or changes do you need to make to live like a disciple of Jesus?

4. **Read Ephesians 5:8–13.** What do you think it means to "live as children of the light"? Why is this so important? In what ways are you choosing to live in the light? If you aren't sure of any yet, consider time alone with God in prayer and seek the Holy Spirit's strength to trust letting go. Make note of an area you still feel kept in the dark.

**5.** **Read John 8:31–32.** According to Jesus, what is the mark of a true disciple? How has the truth set you free in your own life?

**6.** Lisa wrote her own Truth Manifesto (chapter seven) for all of those moments when she is tempted to hide again. Write a few sentences of your own Truth Manifesto to help you keep from hiding. Remind yourself of the uncomplicated life you get to live when you choose honesty over hiding. What encouragement will you need to hear when you're tempted to hide? What verses most inspire you?

**Take Action:** We can make a ton of changes to simplify our lives on the outside, but if we're not willing to be honest, our life will stay complicated—especially on the inside. Jesus lived a truth-filled life of simplicity, and he offers the same to us if we're willing to choose him over everything, including our desire to hide. When we come out of hiding, we choose to trust that God has a better plan. Let's take that step together today. Even if you consider yourself an honest person, there may be areas of life you're still hiding. Here are some of the most common symptoms of hiding:

- living below your potential
- stuck in a cycle of addiction that has altered you mentally and emotionally
- living with a different persona instead of your true self
- walking around depressed and hopeless—without the joy God promises
- struggling physically due to unhealthy choices for your body
- posting pictures on social media to control how others perceive you
- hiding receipts or new purchases from your spouse
- fixated on the perception of everything in your life instead of sharing your reality
- lying about the health of your relationships
- slightly altering the details when you tell a story

The point here is to help you choose honesty over hiding in every area of your life, even in the small stuff. So let's start by telling the truth about something you've been hiding.

THE TRUTH I NEED TO TELL THIS WEEK IS:

_____

**Pray:** Take a few moments to reflect on your answers to the questions and invite God into the ways you want to uncomplicate your life by being *honest*.

## DAY THREE: SHAME VS. MOTIVATION

I want you to choose *real* and *honest* because you truly want to live the Jesus-over-everything kind of life—not because you're embarrassed that other people know about your poor choices or you're afraid of the consequences of those choices. If you're feeling the latter emotions, embarrassed or afraid, then there's a good chance you're feeling shame instead of motivation in your quest to uncomplicate life. And shame is a slippery slope back into the cycle of the *deadly overs*. We need radical promises of hope motivating us, rather than rigid, pointed fingers shaming us. Hope is what woos our hearts to the healthy side of choosing Jesus over everything. As you answer these questions, consider how you can put an end to shame with God's radical promises of hope as your motivation.

**1.** What's behind your desire to uncomplicate your life right now—shame or motivation? Explain why.

**2. Read Psalm 45:10–11.** What is the radical promise of hope in this passage? Name one specific way this promise uncomplicates life for you.

┌─ UNDERSTANDING YOUR BIBLE ─────────────────────────────

# COMMENTARY ON DEUTERONOMY 30:19–20

The mention of witnesses [here in this passage] recalls the form of ancient Near Eastern treaty documents, which have a list of witnesses at the end, often the names of pagan gods. In the biblical covenant, God's creation is called to witness against His people. (*New Geneva Study Bible*)

They shall have life that choose it [NKJV] means they choose the favor of God, and communion with him, shall have what they choose. They that come short of life and happiness, must thank themselves only. They would have had them [life and happiness], if they had chosen them, when they were put to their choice, but they die because they will die. (*Benson*)

—from *New Geneva Study Bible* and *Benson Commentaries*

- **Read:** Also read Psalm 27:1–5 and Deuteronomy 30:4. Note the kind of life God has promised us when we follow him.
- **Look up:** Use your concordance to look up the word *stronghold*. What does this word mean and how is it used throughout Scripture?
- **Explore:** Notice the three encouragements given in Deuteronomy 30:19–20: *Love the Lord God, listen to his voice, hold fast to him*. Consider what it looks like for you to live out these encouragements in your own life.

└────────────────────────────────────────────────────────

**3.** **Read Deuteronomy 30:19–20.** What is the radical promise of hope in this passage? Name one specific way this promise uncomplicates life for you.

**4.** Read Isaiah 43:1–4. What is the radical promise of hope in this passage? Name one specific way this promise uncomplicates life for you.

**5.** Even King David, who knew the promises of God by heart, had to come out of hiding and acknowledge that God was after truth from the inside out in his life (Psalm 51:6). Where do you need to let go of shame by choosing truth from the inside out?

**6.** **Read Jeremiah 17:7–8.** According to the tree metaphor in this passage, what happens when we put our trust in God?

**Take Action:** Here's another Lisa Whittle paraphrase for Jeremiah 17: *Stay connected to Jesus as the source of life . . . there's no need to fear trouble or worry about silence . . . just keep trusting God and doing the work he has for you to do . . . this is the only way to truly succeed.* So, let's connect the dots: *the only way to put Jesus first is by trusting God.* Easy to say, often hard to do. Consider an area of your life that you've been hiding or holding on to because of shame, embarrassment, or fear. My prayer for you is that God's radical promises of hope are enough to help you make the intentional choice to trust God with that specific area.

I WILL CHOOSE TO TRUST GOD WITH THIS AREA OF MY LIFE:

_____

**Pray:** Take a few moments to reflect on your answers to the questions and your action step by inviting God into your desire to trust him out of motivation rather than shame.

# GOING DEEPER (IF YOU WANT MORE)

**Read Mark 5:21–34.** For twelve years, this woman was forced to the fringe of society because she was bleeding. In the Jewish culture of her day, there were strict laws about what women could and could not do while they were bleeding. And this wasn't just the standard cycle of menstrual bleeding (heaven help us all). This was *twelve straight years* of bleeding. Can you imagine? It's amazing this woman was even alive at this point, or that she had enough strength to walk up to Jesus in the middle of the crowd. And yet, somehow, she knew she needed Jesus to uncomplicate her life. I love how Jesus turns around and asks the question, *"Who touched me?"* when he already knew the answer because he's God! But I suspect Jesus wanted to publicly acknowledge this woman's desire to place her faith in him at that moment. Jesus gave her the dignity she was denied due to twelve years of being considered "unclean." And he's willing to do the same for you and me too. Jesus doesn't care how long we've been in hiding, and he already knows why we've been in hiding, so it's time to come clean.

Spend extra time in prayer today as you consider how Jesus' interaction with the bleeding woman relates to your life and your situation today. Perhaps you need to be reminded that God sees you, knows you, and still loves you. And the only way forward with choosing *real over pretty* and *honesty over hiding* is to place your trust in God by putting Jesus first.

**Use this space to jot down notes or thoughts as they come to mind.**

**For Next Week:** Review chapters two and seven in *Jesus Over Everything* and use the space below to write any insights or questions from your personal study that you want to discuss at the next group meeting. The teaching for session three comes from chapters three and five in *Jesus Over Everything*.

# SERVING PEOPLE

LOVE THE LORD YOUR GOD WITH ALL YOUR HEART AND WITH ALL YOUR SOUL AND WITH ALL YOUR MIND AND WITH ALL YOUR STRENGTH. . . . LOVE YOUR NEIGHBOR AS YOURSELF.

MARK 12:30–31 NIV

# WELCOME

Some of us want to be the kind of person who draws people in rather than pushes them away. Sometimes we think that drawing people in has something to do with the gifts we give, or the way we keep a pretty home, or the smart things we have to say. But the truth is that people are drawn in when they feel *safe*. Making someone feel safe is how we make someone feel loved. It's the presence of love that calms fear, draws in the skeptics, brings the prodigals back, and changes the hardest of hearts. Judgment will never do that. Love comes from a place of safety, while judgment comes from a place of fear. God's love is bigger than life and bigger than any fear, and he's invited us into his love.

As image-bearers of God (Genesis 1:26–27), we get to *receive* his love, *give* his love, and *be* his love. We become more like God when we actively take on his character. And nothing speaks more to the character of God than serving other people with the love of God. This is also how we grow and change and become the person we were created to be: *by loving and serving others*. But we have a frustrating habit of getting in our own way. We choose pride over humility, fear over love, fame over service, and then our priorities get all mixed up. We start to believe lies about what makes us successful, or lovable, or popular, or safe. That's why what we're talking about today is so crucial, because it cuts to the core of our identity in Christ and our desire to place Jesus over everything.

Let's take a closer look together as we continue to uncomplicate our life and put Jesus first by choosing *service over the spotlight* and *love over judgment*.

# SHARE

*Briefly discuss one of the following statements:*

- Share what comes to mind when you think of the word *service*.

— or —

- Name *one* area of life where you want to express more love and less judgment.

# READ

*Invite someone to read aloud the following passage as "heart prep" for Lisa's teaching. Listen for fresh insights as you hear the verses being read, and then briefly discuss the questions that follow.*

## THE PARABLE OF THE GOOD SAMARITAN

On one occasion an expert in the law stood up to test Jesus. "Teacher," he asked, "what must I do to inherit eternal life?" "What is written in the Law?" he replied. "How do you read it?" He answered, "'Love the Lord your God with all your heart and with all your soul and with all your strength and with all your mind'; and, 'Love your neighbor as yourself.'" "You have answered correctly," Jesus replied. "Do this and you will live." But he wanted to justify himself, so he asked Jesus, "And who is my neighbor?" In reply Jesus said: "A man was going down from Jerusalem to Jericho, when he was attacked by robbers. They stripped him of his clothes, beat him and went away, leaving him half dead. A priest happened to be going down the same road, and when he saw the man, he passed by on the other side. So too, a Levite, when he came to the place and saw him, passed by on the other side. But a Samaritan, as he traveled, came where the man was; and when he saw him, he took pity on him. He went to him and bandaged his wounds, pouring on oil and wine. Then he put the man on his own donkey, brought him to an inn and took care of him. The next day he took out two denarii and gave them to the innkeeper. 'Look after him,' he said, 'and when I return, I will reimburse you for any extra expense you may have.' "Which of these three do you think was a neighbor to the man who fell into the hands of robbers?" The expert in the law replied, "The one who had mercy on him." Jesus told him, "Go and do likewise." (Luke 10:25–37 NIV)

**What is one key insight that stands out to you from this passage?**

**What was so "good" about the Good Samaritan?**

As you listen to Lisa's teaching, consider where you want freedom from desiring to be in the spotlight instead of serving, or from being judgmental instead of loving others.

# WATCH

*Play the video segment for session three. As you watch, use the following outline to record any thoughts or concepts that stand out to you.*

## NOTES

### The gas station restroom

Asking God for clarity

The cleaning

### Acts of service

*"Service wasn't what Jesus did; it was who he was."*

*"The spotlight is maybe what we crave, but service is what changes us into the best people."*

## Serving others transforms us, it renews us

2 Corinthians 4:16–17

The Jesus-over-everything life is ongoing and daily

The reality about serving

## Lies: Satan is always at the root of lies and deceit

Ezekiel 28:11–19 (in part)

The lies we believe about service

## The spotlight

*"The spotlight in the kingdom on anyone but Jesus doesn't even make sense."*

*"The pedestal belongs to [Jesus] and we belong underneath that pedestal."* –Scott Sauls, pastor and leader

## Service is the Jesus-over-everything way

Questions to ask yourself:

- How easy is it to try to get and to keep people's attention, and to stay on top?
- How good does it feel to be cared about only for our connections or what we can do for someone else?
- How successful are we if we only develop the character that comes from being isolated on a pedestal?

### Serving Jesus out of the overflow of love

When we choose to love God, he gives us the strength to love others.

Matthew 22: *The Greatest Commandment*

Revelation 2

### Service accompanies our love for Jesus

# DISCUSS

*Take a few minutes with your group members to discuss what you just watched and explore these concepts in Scripture.*

1. Who in your life has loved Jesus and served others well, just as Lisa's mom loved Jesus and served her dad? How has your life been influenced by this example?

2. **Read Matthew 20:20–28.** This is how Jesus defines service in light of the desire to focus on ourselves. What does Jesus say is the key to becoming great? In what area of life are you most tempted to elevate yourself: *work, neighborhood/community, friendships, marriage, parenting, extended family, school, church,* etc.? Identify and share how this choice has inhibited you from experiencing Jesus more deeply.

3. Have you ever had an experience like Lisa's friend Debbie, in which you sensed God asking you to serve in a way that was out of your comfort zone or didn't really seem to make sense? Briefly share your experience. Did you choose to follow his prompting? Why or why not, and what was the outcome? Consider both emotional and literal/physical outcomes.

**4.** **Read Philippians 2:3–5.** How does loving God and placing Jesus first help you to love others when you're tempted to judge them? Share an example with the group. If judgment is something you struggle with, consider Jesus' response to all our sins and shortcomings—he loves us. Share a circumstance in your life right now where can you choose to respond in love rather than in judgment?

**5.** Describe to the group a time you served someone else and what the outcome was. How did God use that experience to transform you?

**6.** Share one word to describe what it would feel like to completely humble yourself and choose love over judgment in your relationships with others.

# PRAY

*Pray as a group before you close your time together. Use this space to keep track of prayer requests and group updates.*

# BETWEEN-SESSIONS PERSONAL STUDY

By now you know the deal, but let me say it again. This week, start your *Jesus Over Everything* personal study by spending some time with God each day. Reflect on the material you covered during your group time by engaging in any or all of the following between-sessions exercises. Be sure to read the reflection questions before starting the daily studies and make a few notes in your guide about the experience as you explore what it means to live a Jesus-over-everything kind of life. Remember, the primary goal of these between-sessions studies is for your own spiritual growth and personal reflection, not so that you have the perfect answer for group discussion. And if you haven't done so already, let me encourage you to read chapters three and five of *Jesus Over Everything*.

## WEEKLY REFLECTION: SESSION THREE

*Briefly review your video notes for session three. In the space below, write down the most significant point you took away from this session.*

Reflect on the word you chose at the end of the group session—the word that comes to mind when you think about taking the focus off ourselves and stopping comparisons. List two or three *specific* ways that word will influence your decisions and actions this week as you put Jesus over everything else.

## DAY ONE: SERVICE OVER SPOTLIGHT

If you had the opportunity to have dinner with your favorite musician, author, or movie star, would you do it? My guess is your answer is yes, and mine would be too. And yet, every day we have the opportunity to be in community with the *greatest servant who ever lived*, and some of us are still hesitant to make the most of that opportunity. Have you ever thought about it that way before?

Ready or not, the invitation to serve in the name of Jesus is always available to us. This means every waking moment is an opportunity to choose *service with Jesus over the spotlight*. Not in a way that denies God-given gifts and opportunities or gives toxic-behaving folks the right to boss us around or run over our boundaries (serving God's way doesn't require or facilitate that kind of behavior), but in a way that we take on the activity (mentally and physically) of becoming less so he can become more. Without a heart for true service, we remain self-focused. When we are all about ourselves, we cannot be about God too—these two realities cannot co-exist. One reality has to fade so the other can shine brightly.

Let's take a closer look at the lies we believe about the focus being on us rather than on Jesus as we continue to uncomplicate our lives. My hope in doing this exercise is that you shift the spotlight from yourself to God. This is a daily mindset, not a one-and-done exercise.

Consider how focusing on yourself above all else affects your life. Think about real-life examples of when you've put yourself over others and over God. Fill in the blank boxes at the bottom to identify and reckon with where you need to.

## SERVICE OVER SPOTLIGHT

| Self-Focus vs. Service | How has putting yourself first affected your service to others? Choose one word to describe how self-focus has hindered this area of your life. | How has putting yourself first affected your relationship with God? Choose one word to describe how God sees you in those moments of self-focus. |
|---|---|---|
| **Relationships** When I focus on my own needs vs. the needs of others | | |
| **Work** When I focus on my own task vs. what's best for the greater good | | |
| **Home** When I focus on what I need to relax and recharge vs. what we all need as a family | | |
| **Church** When I focus on what I can get out of church vs. what I can give | | |
| **Community** When I focus on what I want to do vs. what's needed in our community | | |

| Small Group/ Bible Study When I focus on what I think we should learn vs. what God wants to teach us | | |
|---|---|---|
| | | |

Jesus redefined what it means to live a life of service by being the greatest servant of all. He served all of humanity by his life, his death on the cross, and his resurrection. Consider the examples where Jesus served others throughout Scripture, and let those examples be an inspiration to you.

| Examples of Service | What kind of service takes place in this passage? | What opportunity do I have to serve others in this same way? How will this uncomplicate life if I choose to serve like this? |
|---|---|---|
| Matthew 9:18–26 | | |
| Matthew 15:29–39 | | |
| Matthew 25:35–36 | | |
| Mark 15:42–47 | | |
| Luke 10:25–37 | | |
| Luke 10:38–42 | | |
| John 3:1–17 | | |

# COMMENTARY ON 1 PETER 4:10–11

The word "gift" here means "endowment" of any kind, but especially conferred by the Holy Spirit. Here it seems that every kind of endowment (*charisma* in Greek) by which we can do good to others. It does not refer here particularly to the ministry of the word—though it is applicable to that, and includes that—but to all the gifts and graces by which we can contribute to the welfare of others. All this is regarded as a gift, or *charisma*, of God. It is not owing to ourselves, but is to be traced to Him. Regard what you *have* and *have not* as a gift bestowed upon you by God for the common good, and be ready to impart it as the needs of others require. Meaning, in whatever God has favored us more than others, we should be ready to minister [counsel, advise, supply] to their needs. Regarding yourself as the mere stewards of God; that is, as appointed by him to do this work for him, and entrusted by him with what is needful to the benefit of others. He intends to do them good, but he means to do it through your instrumentality, and has entrusted to you as a steward what he designed to confer on them. This is the true idea, in respect to any special endowments of talent, property, or grace, which we may have received from God. [God's] favors are not confined to one single thing; as, for example, to talent for doing good by preaching; but are extended to a great many things by which we may do good to others—influence, property, reputation, wisdom, experience. All these are to be regarded as his gifts; all to be employed in doing good to others as we have opportunity.

–from Barnes' Notes on the Bible Commentary

- **Read:** Romans 12:3–8. Consider what this passage says about the role of each member of the body of Christ.
- **Look up:** Look up *gifts* in your concordance. Take note of how gifts were talked about and exercised among the early Christians.
- **Explore:** Have you ever stopped to consider the idea that God created you with a specific role in mind for his kingdom? You get to serve God by serving others in a unique way with your gifts and talents.

**Read 1 Peter 4:10–11.** It's easy to get caught in the comparison trap even in the way we serve others and serve God. We all have that friend who comes through with the gourmet meal in a moment of crisis. But it's okay if that's not you. This passage reminds us that we have different gifts and talents with which to serve. Serving isn't about being all things to all people. It's about giving and loving and serving with the best of what we've been given. God's given me (Lisa) the gift of discernment, so I serve others well when I pay attention to what God is saying to me on their behalf and I share it with them. How about you? What gifts have you received from God to serve others well? And how are you serving God with the gifts he gave you?

**Take Action:** I get a lot of questions about what it means to *serve*. Here's a quick response: *let the life of Jesus be your example and pay attention to the nudges you get when something catches your attention.* It doesn't require a long definition, and places to serve will vary due to circumstance and opportunity. When you put Jesus first and follow his example, he will be your guide. So pay attention to the nudge, or pause for a moment of prayer and ask Jesus where he wants you to serve today.

THIS WEEK I AM SENSING A NUDGE TO SERVE BY:

_____

**Pray:** Take a few moments to reflect on your answers to the questions and invite God into the ways you want to uncomplicate your life by following his example as the greatest servant of all.

## DAY TWO: LOVE OVER JUDGMENT

We've all been judged a fair share in our life—I, myself, have been judged because of my family, judged because of my blunt personality, judged because of the stance I take on certain issues, judged because of mistakes from my past. But I've done my fair share of judging too, and I bet we have that in common as well.

Here's what I know to be true: *judgment often comes from a place of fear.* When we fear something, we judge it. By turning our fear into judgment, we quickly release our angst or transfer it onto someone or something else—the immediate goal—because none of us wants to sit with our fear(s). But discharging it in the form of judgment only passes it on . . . it doesn't stop it. Judgment makes us feel worse in the long run and only serves to complicate our lives with more baggage.

On the flip side, we love what makes us feel safe. Hear that? Love = safety, judgment = fear. Have you ever connected the dots between those feelings and emotions before this session? We love those who help us feel safe and known and cared for; this is the reward of love. That's why the love of Jesus has always been a safe place for me. And, according to *The Greatest Commandment* in Matthew 22, it is our responsibility to share this safe love of God with others. All throughout the New Testament, Jesus loved others by making them feel safe. And now we get to do the same. Consider your answers to the questions below as we discuss *love over judgment*.

1. Briefly review your reflections from the last between-session exercise on *service over spotlight*. Consider the ways your choice to seek the spotlight for yourself feeds into the cycle of judging others. Describe a circumstance where judgment has kept you from loving another.

2. How have you been impacted by the judgment of others? What fears do you think might have been lurking behind their judgment?

3. **Read Matthew 7:1–6.** What does Jesus say about judgment here? Why do you think he uses such strong language in this passage?

---

UNDERSTANDING YOUR BIBLE

# WHAT DOES THE WORD *JUDGE* MEAN?

In the original Greek, *judge* means: Properly, to distinguish; i.e., decide; by implication, to try, condemn, punish.

κρίνετε / krinete

This word and various forms of this word appear throughout the New and Old Testament. Originally meant *"to separate"* in ancient Greek (used by Homer in *The Iliad*, v, 501), this word was eventually translated as *"to distinguish, to pick out, to be of opinion, to judge."*

–from Strong's 2919 and Wikipedia

- **Read:** Also read Proverbs 9:7–9. What happens when you judge or rebuke the unwise versus the wise?
- **Look up:** Jesus uses the illustration of throwing pearls to pigs. Consider why he uses this specific illustration. If you're not sure, look it up.
- **Explore:** Consider what it means for you to speak love, truth, and grace without judgment. What reason does Jesus give for why we should let him be the Judge?

---

**4.** **Read John 15:9–13.** How have you been impacted by the love of Jesus and the love of others?

**5.** **Read 1 John 4:7–21.** Notice what Jesus has to say about love and fear. According to this passage, what happens to fear when love is present? How do we *know* God's perfect love? How do we *show* God's perfect love?

**6.** Contrary to what many of us believe about Jesus, he did not come into this world to judge us, but rather to save us (John 12:47 NIV). He was born in a smelly manger. He spent time with the sick, the poor, the outcasts of society. He wandered from town to town to share the goodness of God without a place to call home. He washed the dirty feet of his disciples. He died a criminal's death on a wooden cross. Those actions were fueled by love, not fear.

Think about how you've acted toward the people closest to you this week and jot down a few instances here. Were your actions fueled by love or judgment/fear? If they were driven by judgment/fear, what steps will you take to make amends and confess how this hurt someone, even if that someone was ultimately you because you distrusted God?

**Take Action:** We've already identified one way we can take action this week—by making amends for our judgmental actions toward others. But I also want you to consider a proactive mindset as you move from fear and judgment to love. Consider the ways you feel loved by Jesus and by your people on a consistent basis. Now think about how you can do the same for someone in your community: a neighbor, coworker, stranger you meet at the store, classmate, teammate, and so on. And don't forget the people closest to you. Sometimes we assume they *know* we love them, when they actually long for us to *show* we love them.

I WILL CHOOSE TO SHOW LOVE OVER JUDGMENT
TO SOMEONE IN MY COMMUNITY THIS WEEK BY:

_____

**Pray**: Take a few moments to reflect on your answers to the questions and invite God into the ways you want to uncomplicate your life by choosing *love over judgment*.

## DAY THREE: BECAUSE HE FIRST LOVED US

Here's something we often miss: at the end of the day, choosing to love someone and serve someone isn't about us . . . it isn't even about them; *it's actually about Jesus*. It's how we respond to the love we've been so freely given. It's how we allow God to transform our hearts and change our attitudes to be more like Christ. It's the reward of accepting God's love for us. It's how we step fully into our identity as image-bearers of God (Genesis 1:26–27). We have the opportunity to love because he first loved us. We have the opportunity to serve because he first served us. I can't say it more plainly than that. As you answer these questions, consider how God's love through Jesus motivates you toward a lifestyle of love and service—an act of worship to God when you place Jesus first in your life.

1. During the teaching for this session, Lisa shared about the love her mom had for her dad and the rest of their family. It was a deep love that Lisa didn't understand, until she realized her mom loved and served her dad so well because she was really loving and serving Jesus the whole time. Is there an example from someone in your own life who has loved and served others out of their love for Jesus? How has this example impacted you and the way you love others?

2. Is there a particular act of love or service you know God is asking you to do, but you're struggling to move to action? How would that act of love or service make life better for someone else?

**3.** **Read 1 John 4:4.** *The one who is in you is greater.* Say that over and over again (even long after this study is over) until it begins to truly settle in your heart. Who in your life needs to experience the great love of God through your loving presence or acts of service? What can you do to show God's greater love to them?

**4.** **Read John 3:16.** How has God's act of love through Jesus made a difference for you? How have you been *loved, served, rescued, healed, redeemed, freed,* and *found* because of Jesus?

**5.** **Read 1 Corinthians 13.** At times, we're at a loss for what it looks like to love or serve someone well, especially when we struggle with the relationship or we don't really know the person. The Apostle Paul gives us a great guide for loving well in this passage. List the ways you can love and serve others according to these verses:

**6.** God *can* and *will* do greater things through you than the things he did through Jesus. He says so in **John 14:12–14.** Do you really believe this? What changes do you need to make to live your life like this is true?

# COMMENTARY ON 1 CORINTHIANS 13

Using intentional exaggeration, Paul emphasizes the uselessness of gifts exercised without love. Paul personifies love as a person who acts in the ways Christians should imitate. The total picture suggests a description of Christ Himself. Considering the kinds of problems this epistle addresses, these verses are a rebuke to the Corinthians, who were failing to conduct themselves in love. The text also suggests strongly that Paul is referring to the Second Coming of Christ as the final event in God's plan of redemption and revelation. In comparison with what we will receive then, the present blessings are only partial and thus imperfect. It is therefore a sign of immaturity for the Corinthians to treat the temporary, incomplete gifts of the Spirit as hav[ing] ultimate significance.

–from *New Geneva Study Bible*

- **Read:** Jeremiah 31:3. How does this reference to *love* in the Old Testament correlate to the reference to love in 1 Corinthians 13?
- **Look up:** Consider other places the word *love* appears in Scripture, particularly in the Old Testament. What kind of patterns do you see?
- **Explore:** How does God's love for us shape and mold the way we love others?

**Take Action:** Love and service can be one in the same, and they can be two separate things. At the end of the day, if we're really going to live a life of love and service *because of* Jesus, then we need to live this kind of life *with* Jesus. We cannot do these things without Jesus. If we want to live the Jesus-over-everything life, we have to move past our self-interests to the interest of others by putting Jesus first.

BECAUSE OF GOD'S LOVE FOR ME, I WILL LOVE AND SERVE OTHERS TODAY BY: _____

**Pray:** Take a few moments to reflect on your answers to the questions and your action step by inviting God into your desire to love and serve others because he first loved you.

## GOING DEEPER (IF YOU WANT MORE)

**Read John 8:1–11.** Loving and serving others will often look different depending on whom we are loving and serving. Personal growth and spiritual maturity develop when we learn to "read the room" and figure out how to love or serve someone well, based on what they need in the moment. And we see Jesus do this so masterfully in this passage with the woman caught in sin. Jesus knew when to be silent and when to speak up. He knew when to look up and when to look down.

I've even heard some scholars debate the idea that it's not important to know what Jesus was writing on the ground; it's important to understand that Jesus was drawing the eyes of the stone-throwers away from the woman, who may have been standing half-clothed or naked in their midst, by pulling their attention to the ground. If this is true, then there's no doubt Jesus knew how to show an enormous amount of dignity and respect with one small act of love. Jesus also speaks to the idea of judgment when he says, *"Let him who is without sin among you be the first to throw a stone at her."*

If we're going to start throwing stones, we'd better be prepared to receive some stones too. But here's the flip side we so often forget: if we're going to start serving out of love, we need to be willing to receive love too.

Spend extra time in prayer today as you consider how Jesus loves you with the same love he shows to this woman. Jesus not only loves you, he wants *you* to love you too. That's why he says, *"Love your neighbor as you love yourself."* We cannot love others well if we do not love ourselves well. And we cannot love ourselves well without the help and love of Jesus. It's as complicated and simple as that. As you pray, allow yourself to feel the love of Jesus wash over you.

**Use this space to jot down notes or thoughts as they come to mind.**

**For Next Week:** Review chapters three and five in *Jesus Over Everything* and use the space below to write any insights or questions from your personal study that you want to discuss at the next group meeting. The teaching for session four comes from chapters six and eight in *Jesus Over Everything*.

# REMEMBERING WHAT'S TRUE

LISTEN TO MY INSTRUCTION AND
BE WISE; DO NOT DISREGARD IT.

PROVERBS 8:33 NIV

# WELCOME

*Leader, read aloud to the group*

Today we're talking about the importance of not getting caught up in the hype or impulsivity of a culture that constantly wants to push us toward flashy, easy, bigger, and more. And here's the hard truth: Christians are among the worst at buying into this kind of hype. We have a real penchant to outdo or one-up each other, or to heighten spiritual experiences to "out-experience the last thing we did," all in the name of Jesus.

But it's not just what we do to each other as Christians; it's what we do in ourselves trying to fill a God-sized void. Everywhere we turn, we're faced with opportunities to impulsively buy things we don't need to fill spaces we don't use. Many of us are so far into this way of living, we have no clue it's even a problem. Hype pulls us out of the steady disciplines of long-term faithfulness and disrupts a life of wisdom devoted to God and only God.

When we anchor ourselves in the truth of who Jesus is and what the gospel is really about, we're less tempted to give up so easily and have more courage to stay steady. Hype, the never-ending-vacuum of worldly knowledge, complicates our lives. Steadiness and wisdom uncomplicate our lives in a way our hearts truly crave. Let's dig into this together.

# SHARE

*Briefly discuss one of the following statements:*

- Share one thing you did in the "Take Action" section of last week's between-sessions personal study. How has this made a difference for you as you put Jesus first?

— or —

- Share the details of your last impulsive internet purchase. What was it and what made you give in to the impulse?

# READ

*Invite someone to read aloud the following passage as "heart prep" for Lisa's teaching. Listen for fresh insights as you hear the verses being read, and then briefly discuss the questions that follow.*

## JESUS PREDICTS PETER'S DENIAL AND PETER DISOWNS JESUS

Then Jesus told them, "This very night you will all fall away on account of me, for it is written: 'I will strike the shepherd, and the sheep of the flock will be scattered.' But after I have risen, I will go ahead of you into Galilee." Peter replied, "Even if all fall away on account of you, I never will." "Truly I tell you," Jesus answered, "this very night, before the rooster crows, you will disown me three times." But Peter declared, "Even if I have to die with you, I will never disown you." And all the other disciples said the same.

Now Peter was sitting out in the courtyard, and a servant girl came to him. "You also were with Jesus of Galilee," she said. But he denied it before them all. "I don't know what you're talking about," he said. Then he went out to the gateway, where another servant girl saw him and said to the people there, "This fellow was with Jesus of Nazareth." He denied it again, with an oath: "I don't know the man!" After a little while, those standing there went up to Peter and said, "Surely you are one of them; your accent gives you away." Then he began to call down curses, and he swore to them, "I don't know the man!" Immediately a rooster crowed. Then Peter remembered the word Jesus had spoken: "Before the rooster crows, you will disown me three times." And he went outside and wept bitterly. (Matthew 26:31–35, 69–75 NIV)

**What is one key insight that stands out to you from this passage?**

**Why do you think Peter denied Jesus, even when Jesus warned Peter he would do so, and Peter adamantly declared to be loyal to Jesus?**

As you listen to Lisa's teaching, consider where you want freedom from the cultural hype around you, or how could you use some godly wisdom to make better decisions.

# WATCH

*Play the video segment for session four. As you watch, use the following outline to record any thoughts or concepts that stand out to you.*

## NOTES

### Hype and impulsivity

Remember these two core truths:

**1.** Jesus doesn't need our fancy words or tactics to present the gospel to be exciting.

**2.** The Bible is always relevant and always true.

### Remembering what's true: *wisdom and steadiness*

**Satan tempted Jesus in the wilderness, yet Jesus resisted him**

**The draw of hype**
- Personal and popular opinion vs. conviction of the Word

**"YOUR AUTHORITY IS THE WORD OF GOD."**

- The lure of upward mobility (Henri Nouwen)

**"THE LURE TO BE RELEVANT,
SPECTACULAR, AND POWERFUL"**

**Luke 4:1–13: Jesus in the Wilderness**

**1.** Satan tempted Jesus to be <u>relevant</u> by turning stones into bread—making productivity the main point.

**2.** Satan tempted Jesus to be <u>spectacular</u> by setting him on the pinnacle of the temple—making the idea of being someone special the main point.

(Psalm 139)

**3.** Satan tempted Jesus to be <u>powerful</u> by asking Jesus to worship him—giving Jesus dominion over all Satan showed him.

**Jesus resisted by staying:**

- steady
- solid
- confirmed in what he knew
- by holding true to God

The way we counter our culture is by following his lead

**The two most important things to remember:**

- Jesus is enough.
- The Bible is our source for everything.

Jesus shows rage over hype in the temple (Matthew 21:12–13)

The work of Jesus (Matthew 21:14)

Why it's important to remember what's true—remembering *who* is true

**Don't miss out on the amazing life God has for us by remembering what is true: Jesus, the Bible, the gospel.**

# DISCUSS

*Take a few minutes with your group members to discuss what you just watched and explore these concepts in Scripture.*

**1.** Which area of hype makes you most tempted to throw wisdom out the window: the need to be (a) *relevant*, (b) *spectacular*, or (c) *powerful*?

2. Has there ever been a time you've felt you needed to use fancy prayers, words, or displays of the gospel to make it more appealing to someone? Or on the flip side, that you needed to put a little extra "world" into the passage you're reading or quoting to make it more appealing? Why do we do this?

3. What makes the Bible always relevant and always true?

4. How have you experienced others leading with wisdom and steadiness in a way that's countercultural to today's hype and impulsivity?

5. Name a few other examples from Jesus' life where he exhibits wisdom and steadiness.

6. Share one word that describes what it would feel like if you felt steady and stable despite the constant flux of the culture around you.

# PRAY

*Pray as a group before you close your time together. Use this space to keep track of prayer requests and group updates.*

# BETWEEN-SESSIONS PERSONAL STUDY

Be sure to read the reflection questions before you begin the daily studies and make a few notes in your guide about the experience as you explore what it means to live a Jesus-over-everything kind of life. And if you haven't done so already, let me encourage you to read chapters six and eight of *Jesus Over Everything*.

## WEEKLY REFLECTION: Session Four

*Briefly review your video notes for session four. In the space below, write down the most significant point you took away from this session.*

Reflect on the word you chose at the end of the group session—the word that comes to mind when you think about not having to live up to the hype or impulsivity of our culture anymore. List two or three *specific* ways that the Word will influence your decisions and actions this week as you put Jesus over everything else.

## DAY ONE: STEADY OVER HYPE

I'm outing it right now: hype is merely "smoke and mirrors" based on emotions rather than faith or facts. Only when we see hype for what it really is—the pull we feel toward the *spectacular, materially relevant, and what's currently popular*—can we settle into the right mindset about Jesus, the Word, and our role as believers. This leads us to the steady life. The steady life without all the hype may feel understated, but it is the very life of Christ. (And isn't a simpler life without pretentious complications what we really want?) This kind of life honors God while aligning us with God's good and perfect will for our life.

The steadier we are in our spiritual life, the stronger our ability to resist the temptations of the latest cultural hype. But the reality is that the closer aligned our lives become with Jesus, any other way of life loses its attraction and temptation, and we ultimately lose interest in cultural hype altogether.

Let me be clear, cultural hype isn't just the latest internet craze or what's trending on social media. Hype happens in our churches too. The fact that I can even say the words *Christian celebrity* together, and most of you know what I'm talking about, means there are no boundaries to the pervasive hype we experience every day, Christian or not. After all, we are still human, which means we're prone to finding every possible way to justify our own search for the spectacular. But I assure you, hype is shallow and empty. Steadiness is fulfilling and grounding—it leads the way to discipleship, the Jesus-over-everything kind of life.

Let's take a closer look together as we continue to uncomplicate our life and put Jesus first by choosing *steadiness over hype.*

Consider how cultural hype (the pull we feel toward the *spectacular*, *relevant*, and *popular* with the majority) affects your everyday life. Using the chart below, note areas where you feel the most pressure to give in to the hype. Fill in the blank boxes at the bottom with other areas of pressure that come to mind.

## STEADY OVER HYPE

| Areas where I feel the pressure of hype—to be spectacular, relevant, or popular | Real-life examples | What complication is this causing me in honoring God? |
|---|---|---|
| Personal Appearance | | |
| Sex Life | | |
| Family & Friendships | | |
| Work | | |
| Spirituality | | |
| Social Media | | |
| Church | | |
| | | |
| | | |
| | | |
| | | |

Now consider how the choice to be steady in those same areas can make a huge difference for you and your journey to uncomplicate life. Remember, *steady is not stale*. Steadiness allows us to align ourselves to God's will, and allows God to do his best work in us. The steadiness of God is also what allows us to navigate the pain and unpredictability of our lives.

| Today, I choose steady over hype | Real-life examples of how I will do this | How will this uncomplicate my life? |
| --- | --- | --- |
| Personal Appearance | | |
| Sex Life | | |
| Family & Friendships | | |
| Work | | |
| Spirituality | | |
| Social Media | | |
| Church | | |
| | | |
| | | |
| | | |
| | | |

┌─ UNDERSTANDING YOUR BIBLE ─────────────────┐

# COMMENTARY ON 1 CORINTHIANS 15:58

Therefore—because all this is so—because there is a life hereafter—let this life here be worthy of it. You might grow weak and faint-hearted if you could think that all your work for God and truth here might be wasted; but it is not so. It cannot be "in vain" if it be "in the Lord." It is very striking and very expressive of the real spirit of the gospel that a chapter which leads us step by step through the calm process of logic, and through glowing passages of resistless eloquence to the sublimest thoughts of immortality, should at last thus close with words of plain and practical duty. Christianity never separates, in precept or in promise, "the life that now is" and "that which is to come."

–from *Ellicott's Commentary for English Readers*

- **Read:** Also read 2 Chronicles 15:7. Consider the similar message of these two passages.
- **Look up:** Some translations of 1 Corinthians 15:58 use the term *steadfast* or *immovable*. What does it mean to be steadfast?
- **Explore:** How does the Christian view of afterlife in heaven shape the way you live your life here and now?

**Read 1 Corinthians 15:58.** This passage explains what it means to be steady. Steadiness is the long and short work of obedience. It's like training for a sprint and a marathon all at the same time. But this work is never in vain. What will it take for you to *stand firm, be steadfast,* and *give yourself fully to the work of the Lord* no matter your circumstances or situation? Where you do you need the help of Jesus to step back from the hype in your life?

**Take Action:** There are times in life when we need to do more than just walk away from the temptation of hype. We actually need to clear the clutter too. Is there a particular relationship that contributes to the allure of hype in your life? If so, consider limiting your time with that person or community. If you're tempted to become a follower by buying into a feel-good message that is contrary to the Word, unsubscribe from the company's emails or unfollow the account on social media.

Does your small group conversation take a quick turn that you know in your spirit isn't God-honoring? Move on. Does your church care more about the production of the weekend service than they do about the spiritual health of the leaders and the congregation or community? Take a break and consider investing your time and energy in a new church community. You get the idea. I'm not here to dictate what choice you will make, I'm just here to call you to some type of action that aligns your life with Jesus in character, compassion, service, and purpose.

THIS WEEK I WILL CLEAR THE CLUTTER OF HYPE BY:

_____

**Pray:** Take a few moments to reflect on your answers to the questions and invite God into the ways you want to uncomplicate your life by choosing *steadiness over hype*.

## DAY TWO: WISDOM OVER KNOWLEDGE

We don't lack for information and available knowledge in our society, which can be a good thing most of the time. But here's the clincher: we can know it all and yet miss what really counts. That's why wisdom is a most precious and powerful gift, different from the exercise of learning that comes from reading and studying information. Wisdom comes with the presence of the Holy Spirit. We receive wisdom when, like King Solomon (1 Kings 3), we ask God for it. In fact, Solomon didn't even use the word *wisdom* when he prayed; rather, he asked God for an "understanding mind . . . to know the difference between right and wrong."

Wisdom is far superior than knowledge and is a gift from God. At the end of the day, Jesus isn't interested in what we know; he's interested in how we live. But for many of us who claim to know Christ, we pursue knowledge over wisdom because it's far easier to learn more *about* God than it is to live with wisdom and discernment *with* God. Choosing wisdom over knowledge takes time, commitment, and discipline.

┌─────────────────────────────────────────────────────────────┐

── UNDERSTANDING YOUR BIBLE ──

# WHAT DOES THE WORD *WISDOM* MEAN?

In the original Hebrew of the Old Testament, *wisdom* means: skill, wisely, wits.

חָכְמַת/ ḥā·ḵə·maṯ

This word and various forms of this word appear 222 times throughout the Old Testament (Hebrew) and the New Testament (Greek). Wisdom was regarded as one of the highest virtues among the Israelites, along with kindness and justice.

–from Strong's 2451 and Wikipedia

- **Read:** Also read Acts 7:22. Solomon's wisdom far exceeded the wisdom of others, which is amazing considering various Scripture and historical references to the wisdom of the ancient Egyptians.
- **Look up:** Look up wisdom in a concordance to learn about more examples of wisdom throughout Scripture. *Hint: Proverbs is full of wisdom about wisdom!*
- **Explore:** Consider what it means for you to ask God for wisdom, and then walk in the ways of wisdom.

└─────────────────────────────────────────────────────────────┘

**1.** Briefly review your reflections from the last between-session exercise on *steady over hype*. Consider whether your impulse to stay relevant feeds into the cycle of hype in your life. As you look over your hype chart, in what area(s) of life do you need wisdom to pursue steadiness?

**2.** Wisdom requires something knowledge doesn't: it requires us to *take action*. Sometimes that action may be the discipline of silence, or even the action of restraint. How have you witnessed someone taking action with wisdom? What did this stir in you or inspire you to do?

**3.** **Read 1 Corinthians 13:1–3, 8–13.** According to this passage, what happens when we have knowledge without wisdom? What else are we lacking? What makes knowledge partial and what makes it complete? In what ways are we childlike in our thinking and how can we mature?

**4.** **Read James 1:22–27.** Wisdom takes the Bible seriously. What does James say about knowledge vs. wisdom (even though he doesn't actually use those words)? What do you think about James' claim that being religious can be hype? Do you resonate with any of the ways James says you can be fooling yourself? Why and in what ways?

**5.** **Read Galatians 5:22–26.** Wisdom also means the ability to self-regulate. This means we exercise the ability to walk away from what we know is not healthy or right. How does this passage define wisdom as "fruit"? According to verse 24, where does our ability to self-regulate come from? Where do you need self-regulation?

**6.** A wise person listens and learns. I have a friend who reminds her kids that the best leaders are "listeners and learners." I agree. What have you learned recently by pausing long enough to listen? What do you think God would say to you if you paused long enough to sit still and listen to him?

**Take Action:** Knowledge requires a search; wisdom requires an ask. I want to challenge you with something very simple today: *ask God for wisdom*. But make sure you're ready to receive it. If you're being influenced more by gurus on your social media feed than you are by the Word of God, you're going to have a hard time receiving the wisdom God has for you. So do what you need to do to clear out the knowledge clutter and let God be your only guide. Then, when you ask for wisdom, get ready to receive it!

THIS WEEK I WILL ASK GOD FOR WISDOM BY:

_____

**Pray:** Take a few moments to reflect on your answers to the questions and invite God into the ways you want to uncomplicate your life by seeking *wisdom over knowledge*.

## DAY THREE: GROWTH OVER IMMATURITY

I briefly mentioned growth over immaturity in chapter six of the book, "Steady Over Hype," but I thought now might be a good time to flesh this out. I'm convinced steadiness and wisdom lead to purposeful longevity which leads to deep and lasting growth. This means we steadily allow Jesus to keep plowing the soil of our lives because we are committed to the longevity of our spiritual lives, marriages, jobs, friendships, and dreams. These are the things that matter, and they take time.

If we give in to the impulse of every bit of hype or every new piece of knowledge that flies our way, we stunt the growth God has for us and we remain immature. The soil of our lives stays overgrown and unplowed because we're not willing to pause and dig deep. Have you ever wondered why there are so many farming metaphors in Scripture? It's because growth takes time, and vegetation is the best example we have to explain the way growth happens. God wants to give us every opportunity he can to make sure we understand that our growth mirrors the growth of the land.

┌─ UNDERSTANDING YOUR BIBLE ─────────────────────────────┐

# COMMENTARY ON JOHN 15:1–8

What suggested this lovely parable of the vine and the branches is equally unimportant and undiscoverable. Many guesses have been made, and, no doubt, as was the case with almost all our Lord's parables, some external object gave occasion for it. It is a significant token of our Lord's calm collectedness, even at that supreme and heart-shaking moment, that He should have been at leisure to observe, and to use for His purposes of teaching, something that was present at the instant. The deep and solemn lessons which He draws, perhaps from some vine by the wayside, are the richest and sweetest clusters that the vine has ever grown. The great truth in this chapter, applied in manifold directions, and viewed in many aspects, is that of the living union between Christ and those who believe on Him, and the parable of the vine and the branches affords the foundation for all which follows.

–from *MacLaren's Expositions*

- **Read:** Hosea 10:1; Matthew 21:33; and Luke 13:6. The vine was a symbol of the ancient church.
- **Look up:** Consider the purpose of Jesus' parables. Look them up in your Bible or online and read through some of these parables.
- **Explore:** What are the common themes of Jesus' parables? What kind of metaphor comes to mind today as you consider your connection to Jesus as your Savior?

└────────────────────────────────────────────────────────┘

God, in all of his glory and wisdom, knows we live our best lives when we bear fruit. It is, in fact, a sign we are actually growing. Immaturity stunts our growth and never allows the fruit in our lives to ripen. Just the thought of biting into unripe fruit puckers my mouth. We can say no to sour and immature. Let's allow God to grow good things in the soil of our lives.

1. How have you sacrificed growth for the sake of hype or impulsivity? How has your own immaturity stunted your opportunities for growth?

2. Often at the root of our choice to choose immaturity over growth is some kind of fear. How has this been true for you? What fear holds you back from growing?

3. **Read John 15:1–8.** According to this passage, what's the key to growth and bearing fruit? How will you pursue this kind of growth?

4. **Read Luke 13:18–19.** Our personal growth isn't always just for us. God often uses growth to influence some*one* or some*thing* else. What else is affected by the growth of the mustard seed in this passage? How is this small detail actually significant considering the ecosystem of a garden?

5. **Read Colossians 1:9–10.** Listen to the way Paul and Timothy care about the growth and wisdom of the people of Colossae. We see that the growth of just one person impacts the community around that person. How do you express your care for the growth of people around you?

**6.** Where do you want or need to grow? In what ways are you pursuing growth in God?

**Take Action:** Growth is a tricky action step to take. Here's why: *we can't actually make ourselves grow.* God makes us grow. We can do the hard work of staying steady, plowing the ground, taking care of the soil, pulling the weeds, clearing the rocks, mending the fences, praying for the proper weather conditions, learning all about the techniques of growth. But ultimately God is responsible for the growth. So do the good work at hand and praise God for any growth that comes as a result.

I WILL TAKE ONE STEP TOWARD GROWTH THIS WEEK BY:

_____

**Pray:** Take a few moments to reflect on your answers to the questions and your action step by inviting God into your desire to choose *growth over immaturity.*

## GOING DEEPER (IF YOU WANT MORE)

**Read Proverbs 8.** The concept of wisdom is somewhat mysterious to me. Especially when I read this passage. But I know God is big enough for all my questions because he's been dealing with my questions for a very long time. Wisdom from a supernatural mind is a mystery to me, yet what I do know is that wisdom is a gift from God, available to a human such as myself . . . such as you, too, according to the Bible.

I can see and feel and maybe even explain to some degree how wisdom shows up in a conversation or in decision-making or in marriage or parenting or leading or in handling finances. But I have a hard time finding the words to define *wisdom*. So I'd love to hear what you think. Read through this passage carefully and slowly. Make note of any and all descriptions of wisdom that stand out to you.

Then spend extra time in prayer today as you consider the gift of wisdom. If all that comes to mind are more questions about wisdom, remember . . . God can handle those.

**Use this space to jot down notes or thoughts as they come to mind.**

**For Next Week:** Review chapters six and eight in *Jesus Over Everything* and use the space below to write any insights or questions from your personal study that you want to discuss at the next group meeting. The teaching for session five comes from chapters four and nine in *Jesus Over Everything*.

# CHANGING YOUR HEART

FOR GOD HAS NOT CALLED US
FOR IMPURITY, BUT IN HOLINESS.

1 THESSALONIANS 4:7 ESV

# WELCOME

*Leader, read aloud to the group.*

We could probably spend a whole weekend retreat together talking about choices from our past we're not proud of and still not have enough time to share all our stories. If your early college years or young adult seasons were anything like mine, there's a good chance you may not even remember some of those poor choices. But our life as a follower of Jesus isn't just about making *good* choices; it's about making the *best* choice. And the best choice is to pursue God.

Our pursuit of God can best be explained by our commitment to holiness. It is the choice that uncomplicates our life because when we pursue life God's way, his way works. And what could be better than an uncomplicated life, ordained by the divine creator? But choosing holiness comes at a cost to our human desires, because the path to holiness requires us to give up our personal freedom and requires long-term commitment over our short-term mood swings. If only we'd understand that choosing holiness over freedom *is* choosing freedom—what comes on the other side of our pursuit of holiness is ultimate *freedom in Christ.*

That's the paradox of a holy life. We give up our personal freedom in order to get greater spiritual freedom. It's hard to put words to that kind of greater freedom unless you've experienced it. And that's the goal of this entire study: to *experience* a life of spiritual dependence on God and a greater freedom than we've ever before known. Some of us have known Jesus for a long time and not yet known the full scope of the joy of what that relationship is meant to be.

Let's take a closer look together as we continue to uncomplicate our life and put Jesus first by choosing *holiness over freedom* and *commitment over mood.*

# SHARE

*Briefly discuss one of the following statements:*

- Share what comes to mind when you think of the word *holiness*.

— or —

- Name *one* area of commitment in your life that requires a lot of focus and attention.

# READ

*Invite someone to read aloud the following passage as "heart prep" for Lisa's teaching. Listen for fresh insights as you hear the verses being read, and then briefly discuss the questions that follow.*

## THE BIRTH OF JOHN THE BAPTIST FORETOLD

In the time of Herod king of Judea there was a priest named Zechariah, who belonged to the priestly division of Abijah; his wife Elizabeth was also a descendant of Aaron. Both of them were righteous in the sight of God, observing all the Lord's commands and decrees blamelessly. But they were childless because Elizabeth was not able to conceive, and they were both very old. Once when Zechariah's division was on duty and he was serving as priest before God, he was chosen by lot, according to the custom of the priesthood, to go into the temple of the Lord and burn incense. And when the time for the burning of incense came, all the assembled worshipers were praying outside. Then an angel of the Lord appeared to him, standing at the right side of the altar of incense. When Zechariah saw him, he was startled and was gripped with fear. But the angel said to him: "Do not be afraid, Zechariah; your prayer has been heard. Your wife Elizabeth will bear you a son, and you are to call him John. He will be a joy and delight to you, and many will rejoice because of his birth, for he will be great in the sight of the Lord. He is never to take wine or other fermented drink, and he will be filled with the Holy Spirit even before he is born. He will bring back many of the people of Israel to the Lord their God. And he will go on before the Lord, in the spirit and power of Elijah, to turn the hearts of the parents to their children and the disobedient to the wisdom of the righteous—to make ready a people prepared for the Lord." (Luke 1:5–17 NIV)

**What is one key insight that stands out to you from this passage?**

**What is so special about Zechariah and Elizabeth? For what reason were they chosen by God to be the parents of John the Baptist?**

As you listen to Lisa's teaching, consider where you want to be more like Jesus, desiring his holiness above your personal freedom and choosing commitment to God over your ever-changing moods.

# WATCH

*Play the video segment for session five. As you watch, use the following outline to record any thoughts or concepts that stand out to you.*

## NOTES
**What it means to be unwell:**

**1.** A lack of commitment

**2.** Doing what *we* want instead of deferring to *God*

**Freedom: we have more freedom in Jesus
than we can ever have on our own**

> "OBEDIENCE IS GOD'S BEST ADVICE TO US
> FOR THE LIFE THAT WE WANT MOST."

**Holiness: the choice to uncomplicate our lives by doing it God's way**

> "COMMITTING TO GOD IS ABOUT A
> LIFESTYLE OF SECURITY."

We don't have to be unwell

Things to consider today:

1. What is distracting me from living *all in* with Jesus?

2. What am I afraid to give up in order to follow him with my whole heart?

**Choosing Jesus over *you***

Joel 2—The Day of the Locust

> "WE FEEL MOST AT RISK WHEN WE'RE IN CRISIS."

Full restoration happens with God

> "COMING CLEAN AND LIVING HOLY WILL
> BENEFIT US FOR THE REST OF OUR LIVES."

Obedience: the way you calm your restless life down

> "THE PROBLEM WITH WESTERN CHRISTIANS IS
> NOT THAT THEY AREN'T WHERE THEY SHOULD
> BE. BUT THAT THEY AREN'T WHAT THEY SHOULD
> BE WHERE THEY ARE." –OS GUINNESS

Our location doesn't matter—Paul in prison

**Freedom: the difference between freedom *from* and freedom *of***

- Freedom *from*—a breaking away; the divorcing of an unhealthy spiritual mindset (Galatians 3:11–12)

- Freedom *of*—a freedom from the grip of sin; freedom of the spirit, living a Spirit-led life (Romans 8:1–4)

**As Christians, we live a life of free will *and* spiritual dependence**

Holiness over freedom is not a freedom from legalism; it's the freedom of the flesh vs. freedom over the spirit:

- Freedom of the flesh—governed by us

- Freedom over the spirit—governed by God

**Holiness is a choice; it's a commitment**

Spiritual disciplines are the routines of Jesus

**Commitment: living life impressed by your commitment
to God rather than someone or something else**

*"A life dictated by the change of the mood is a life wrecked by complications from its instability."*

Genesis 22—Abraham and Isaac

**"EVERY YES TO GOD, SMALL AS IT MAY SEEM, AND EVERY
NO TO OUR OWN FLESH IS TRANSFORMING."**

God can change our hearts so that our hearts long to put *Jesus over everything*.

**Take inventory of your life. Where are you choosing
mood over commitment, freedom over holiness?**

- Anything we use to escape reality or numb ourselves
- Anything that takes us back mentally or keeps us in a sinful state of mind
- Anything that goes against the Word
- Anything that takes time away from the pursuit of holy living
- Anything that mimics or manufactures true joy or fulfillment from Jesus

**Two powerful questions to ask yourself every time you make a decision:**

**1.** Is this a *Jesus-first* choice or a *me-first* choice?

**2.** Will this choice help me become more like Christ?
And then ask God for wisdom for whatever falls through the cracks.

> "THIS IS NOT ABOUT RULES; IT'S ABOUT RENEWAL."

**To become more like Jesus and uncomplicate your life, choose *holiness over freedom* and *commitment over mood*.**

# DISCUSS

*Take a few minutes with your group members to discuss what you just watched and explore these concepts in Scripture.*

**1.** What is your initial response to the concept of choosing *holiness over personal freedom* and *commitment over momentary mood*? Is there someone in your life who models this well? Give a brief example.

**2.** Which area is the bigger struggle for you: are you more tempted to choose your personal freedom over holiness, or let your mood dictate your level of commitment? Why is this a struggle for you? Can you connect where your struggle is complicating your life in and for Christ?

**3.** Together, answer the two questions Lisa asked at the beginning of the session. The first is: What is distracting me from living *all in* with Jesus? Consider distractions we may all face in today's culture, as well as any personal distractions you experience.

**4.** Lisa's second question is: What am I afraid to give up in order to follow Jesus with my whole heart? Why does anything pose more fear than losing a relationship with Jesus? Discuss whether any fear that keeps us from following Christ is rational or irrational and what ways we can overcome or disregard these fears. There is nothing irrational about following Jesus, but our culture may not always agree. How do we deal with it?


**5.** When you inventory the things that keep you from choosing holiness and commitment to Jesus, which "anything" is the most challenging for you right now?


**6.** Share one word to describe what it would feel like if you chose holiness over personal freedom and commitment over your ever-changing mood. Why did you choose this word, and is it realistic to claim this word as truth over your life? Are you committing now to choosing holiness and Jesus over your personal freedom and ever-changing mood?


# PRAY

*Pray as a group before you close your time together. Use this space to keep track of prayer requests and group updates.*

# BETWEEN-SESSIONS PERSONAL STUDY

Be sure to read the reflection questions before beginning the daily studies and make a few notes in your guide about the experience as you explore what it means to live a Jesus-over-everything kind of life. And if you haven't done so already, let me encourage you to read chapters four and nine of *Jesus Over Everything*.

## WEEKLY REFLECTION: SESSION FIVE

*Briefly review your video notes for session five. In the space below, write down the most significant point you took away from this session.*

Reflect on the word you chose at the end of the group session—the word that comes to mind when you think about choosing holiness and commitment. List two or three *specific* ways that word will influence your decisions and actions this week as you put Jesus over everything else.

## DAY ONE: HOLINESS OVER FREEDOM

Many of us are trapped or enslaved by our own freedoms—where we go, what we watch, how we spend our money, how we spend our time. We binge-watch our favorite shows over exercising. We choose financial security and a consistent paycheck over our calling. We choose the one-way ease of online conversations over the two-way complications of real-life relationships. We choose to numb ourselves instead of experience the highs and lows of life. We'd rather escape to avoid anything that feels slightly uncomfortable and out of control. You get the idea. And I'm sure you could keep adding to the list of ways we are enslaved to our own freedoms.

But here's the promise I've experienced in my own life: when you choose *holiness over freedom*, Jesus will give you a greater measure of freedom than you could ever otherwise know. That's the irony of the Christian faith: we live a human life of complete free will and simultaneously a completely dependent spiritual life. I can't force you to believe me nor do I expect you to take my word for it, but I will challenge you to try it. And here's the best part: there's something amazing in it for you. Every time we choose God's way of life, we uncomplicate our own way of life.

TAKE NOTE: WE MOVED THE CHART EXERCISE TO DAY THREE. IF YOU PREFER STARTING OUT WITH A CHART, THEN STAY WITH US. THE REFLECTIVE WORK YOU DO TODAY WILL MATTER TO THE WORK YOU DO IN THE CHART EXERCISE ON DAY THREE OF THIS SESSION.

1. During the teaching session, Lisa dispelled a few myths of personal freedom. But this idea of giving up personal freedom for holiness can still be challenging to embrace. For many of us, this decision hinges on our answer to this question: Do you believe Jesus is for you and that he has your best interests in mind? Why or why not?

┌─ UNDERSTANDING YOUR BIBLE ─────────────────

# COMMENTARY ON ROMANS 8:1–4

The apostle's concern here is pastoral. Paul is telling his readers, in light of the foregoing reminder of their continuing sinfulness, they must now recall their acceptance, immunity and security in Christ. No condemnation [means] probably in both senses—the judgement and the punishment. The law of the Spirit means God's operative power. The law of sin is the operative power of sin, or else the divine law as used by sin to produce death. Paul does not criticize the moral law, but notes once more that because of humanity's sinfulness, it cannot bring salvation. The words "His own son" are reminiscent of the binding of Isaac in Genesis 22:2, and point to the tremendous cost of our redemption. Christ's humanity was like ours in that He could be tempted, and lived his life as a part of a fallen world full of frailty and exposed to vast pressures. But he did not sin, and there was no moral and spiritual corruption in him. Paul seems to be saying in verse three that in the crucifixion . . . sin was judged and condemned so that now all its claims to have us condemned have become invalid. There is no condemnation remaining for those who are in Christ.

–from *New Geneva Study Bible*

- **Read:** Romans 8:10; Corinthians 13:5; and Colossians 1:17. Notice how these passages illuminate the mystical and spiritual union between Christ and believers.
- **Look up:** Use a concordance to look up the attributes of holiness. Make a list and mark three attributes you want to start reflecting in your own life.
- **Explore:** What are the ways holiness contributes to freedom, according to these passages?

**2.** Have you ever done something to "escape" being you or to numb your complicated life? What was it and why did you feel the need to escape?

**3. Read Romans 8:1–4.** The freedom that accompanies holiness isn't earned by following the laws of Scripture (otherwise known as legalism); it's earned by following the Holy Spirit. In what specific ways have you attempted to earn holiness by obeying the law instead of following the Spirit? How did that complicate things for you?

**4. Read 1 Corinthians 10:23–24.** You have the right to do anything—that is your personal freedom. But not everything is helpful to living your best life—that is where holiness comes in. Can you name a situation or decision that was good but not best as it related to your relationship with God? How has that experience informed your choices regarding what's best?

**5. Read Colossians 3:15–17.** According to this passage, what does holiness look like for a community of believers? How have you experienced this kind of community; or if you haven't experienced it, where could you go to find it?

**6.** Our relationship with Jesus is where our liberties (personal freedom) live at peace with our convictions (holiness). Can you honestly say you have that kind of peace in Jesus right now? If not, what liberties or freedoms do you need to let go of and what convictions do you need to embrace?

**Take Action:** I'm sure most of us have, at one time or another, sensed God asking us to let something go, but we've resisted. And there are all sorts of reasons for that resistance, but none of them matter if those reasons are contrary to what we sense from God. Deep down, we know what to do, we just don't want to do it. But God's best is truly our best. If you haven't allowed yourself to experience God's best, what do you have to lose by trying? The promises of God cannot be misleading. Therefore, everything he says in the Word about the freedom on the other side of obedience, surrender, and trust isn't too good to be true: it truly is true.

I WILL CHOOSE HOLINESS TODAY BY LETTING GO OF:

_____

**Pray:** Take a few moments to reflect on your answers to the questions and your action step by inviting God into your desire to choose holiness—God's true freedom—over your own personal freedom.

## DAY TWO: COMMITMENT OVER MOOD

Even though I've studied plenty of Scripture about commitment—and my passion comes from the difference it has made in my own relationship with Jesus—there are still days I waffle between the commitments I've made and my ever-changing mood. But on a practical level, here's how it bites me: every time I cancel plans because I don't "feel" like doing something, I either suffer from guilt or I scramble to reschedule out of obligation (or actual desire), and in the end, things wind up far more complicated than if I'd just kept my commitment to begin with. On the flip side, people cancel on me too, sometimes at the last minute, which causes a completely different kind of angst. Life would be much simpler if we all just stuck to our commitments.

Our relationship with Jesus suffers most because of this issue. The majority of our lack of spending time with him through the years has come from not being in the mood to do it or committing to something instead of him, and I speak from experience. It may have felt harmless at the time, but when we miss out on time with Jesus, we starve the spiritual side of our lives. This is when complications set in. We are less equipped to choose well, deny our moods, and more tempted to choose our personal freedom over his holiness. That's why it's not only wiser, but also easier, to decide ahead of time that feelings don't get to boss us. It's like deciding ahead of time we're going to that 5 a.m. class at the gym. We will *always* choose a warm bed over an early exercise class unless we've committed to that class ahead of time. It's with that same mindset we choose the Jesus-over-everything lifestyle.

1. Briefly review your reflections from the Day One exercise: *holiness over freedom.* Consider the ways your choice for personal freedom feeds into the cycle of choosing your mood over commitment. In what areas of your life have you experienced the most tension between freedom and commitment?

2. Consider your childhood upbringing. What was the perspective of your parents or caregivers regarding the idea of commitment? How has their perspective influenced your view of commitment?

3. **Read Proverbs 16:1–3.** What promise does God give to us as a result of our commitment to him? How has this been true for you?

4. **Read Galatians 6:1–10.** What happens, in a spiritual sense, if we stay committed and do not give up? How have you committed to doing good to all people?

┌─ UNDERSTANDING YOUR BIBLE ─────────────────────────┐

# WHAT DOES THE WORD *COMMIT* MEAN?

In the original Hebrew of the Old Testament, *commit* means: remove, roll away, down, together, run down, seek occasion, trust.

גֹּל / gōl

This word and various forms of this word appear throughout the Old Testament (Hebrew) and the New Testament (Greek). However, this specific word *commit* —as used here in "commit your actions to the Lord" (NLT)—literally means to "roll [your actions] upon Him" because they are a burden too heavy to bear on your own.

—from Strong's Hebrew 1556 and *Ellicott's Commentary for English Readers*

- **Read:** Also read Galatians 6:1–10. This passage talks about the commitment we have to one another in Christ.
- **Look up:** Look up *commit* in a concordance to learn about more examples of *commitment* throughout Scripture.
- **Explore:** Consider what it means for you to commit, or recommit, your life to God and imagine yourself *rolling your burdens upon him*. Also seek out the kind of committed community mentioned in Galatians 6.

└────────────────────────────────────────────────────┘

**5.** **Read Colossians 3:23–24.** How does this passage encourage or inspire your commitment to God?

**6.** How does being committed to Jesus, regardless of your mood, uncomplicate your life? Name a few practical ways this has been true for you.

**Take Action:** I'm sure by now you have a nagging sense of areas in your life where you could be more committed—more committed to Jesus, to your people, and to your priorities—and ruled less by your daily mood. So, let's keep this short and sweet today.

I WILL STICK WITH THIS COMMITMENT TODAY
(OR THIS WEEK) EVEN THOUGH I DON'T FEEL LIKE IT:

_____

**Pray:** Take a few moments to reflect on your answers to the questions and invite God into the ways you want to uncomplicate your life by choosing *commitment over mood*.

## DAY THREE: SPIRITUAL DISCIPLINES

There will be times in our lives when we will still want to choose our personal freedoms over our commitment to holiness. We may battle this issue until the day we die. But most things in the Christian life come down to choices. We can choose to give in to our own personal freedoms or we can choose to give our lives away to Jesus. Choosing Jesus brings far greater benefits of right-living. Giving up our personal freedoms brings holiness, and holiness brings freedom. That's the way it works in the upside-down kingdom of God.

But the choice to choose holiness comes with another choice—the choice to choose holiness again and again and again, each and every day. Holiness requires a committed life of prayer, time in God's Word, and daily dying to our own selfish wants and desires. These are the never-changing disciplines of our faith, also called *spiritual disciplines*. I like to call these "God's guardrails" because they help to keep us on track. Spiritual disciplines guard us from veering off on the slippery slope of compromise. And compromise, especially in the area of personal freedom, leads to complication. It's only when we are weary enough of the complications of our lives that we'll do whatever it takes to declutter our lives.

Let's take a look at how practicing spiritual disciplines uncomplicates our life and helps us chose *holiness over freedom* and *commitment over mood*.

Consider how your personal freedoms have complicated your life. And while doing so, take heart, we will get to the decluttering part soon. Also, if other complicated areas of your life come to mind, fill in the blank boxes at the bottom with those thoughts.

## THE COMPLICATIONS OF PERSONAL FREEDOM

| Areas of Personal Freedom | Real-life examples of decisions that were good for my personal freedom but not best for my spiritual life | What complication has this caused in my life? |
| --- | --- | --- |
| Finances | | |
| Relationships | | |
| Appearance | | |
| Words | | |
| Actions | | |
| Time | | |
| | | |
| | | |
| | | |

I'm 100-percent convinced that spiritual disciplines are the surest way to clear out our hearts and get rid of the complications in our lives. Jesus practiced disciplines while he walked this earth in order to maintain a healthy spiritual connection with God the Father. Jesus prayed; he fasted; he spent time in community; he rested; he retreated; he lived a simple life. And all of those disciplines are readily available to us today. So, take some time to practice a few disciplines this week using the chart below. If practicing spiritual disciplines is normal for you, then take your current disciplines a few steps further or try a new discipline.

## DISCIPLINES THAT DECLUTTER

| Spiritual Disciplines | Real-life examples of how I want to or already participate in these disciplines | How does this uncomplicate my life? |
|---|---|---|
| Prayer | | |
| Silence & Solitude | | |
| Worship | | |
| Spiritual Friendships | | |
| Bible Study | | |
| Simplicity | | |
| Rest | | |

┌─ UNDERSTANDING YOUR BIBLE ─────────────────────────────────┐

# COMMENTARY ON ACTS 2:42

This is a summary of the essential elements needed in Christian discipleship. They are elements the apostles had learned from their experience with Jesus: His teaching about his person and work (Matthew 16:18, 19; Luke 24:46) and their Christian responsibility as his followers (Matthew 5–7); the fellowship of Christ with his disciples (John 13); the Lord's Supper—the breaking of bread (Matthew 26:17–30); and His prayer life and with the disciples (Matthew 6:5; Luke 11:1–13; John 17). Or Ellicott describes this as "the apostles' doctrine"—four elements of the life of the new society are dwelt on. (1) They grew in knowledge of the truth by attending to the teaching of the Apostles . . . (2) They joined in outward acts of fellowship with each other, acts of common worship, acts of mutual kindness and benevolence (what we technically call communion) . . . (3) Breaking of bread, what was afterwards known as the Lord's Supper which took its place as a permanent universal element in the Church's life with baptism . . . (4) Prayer, in like manner, included private as well as public devotions. The use of the plural seems to indicate recurring times of prayer at fixed hours.

—from *New Geneva Study Bible* and *Ellicott's Commentary for English Readers*

- **Read:** Isaiah 58:6–8. This is where the practice of *breaking bread* comes from in ancient Israel. What was promised as a result of sharing bread?
- **Look up:** Use a concordance to look up the term *discipleship*. Where else do these elements emerge in the lives of the early Christians?
- **Explore:** How do you practice discipleship today? What can you do to incorporate these four elements of discipleship into your weekly worship?

└────────────────────────────────────────────────────────────┘

**Read Acts 2:42.** Here we find the basic rhythm of disciplines practiced by early Christians. Their desire to love God (holiness) and know God (commitment) fueled these disciplines. But they too faced the same difficulties and challenges of personal freedom we face today: conflict, temptation, pain, desire, and so on. Throughout the book of Acts are mentions of the disciplines and the development of these disciplines as the believers made space for God and kept company with Jesus. Consider what it would look like to foster this kind of community where spiritual disciplines are practiced together as the norm, rather than the exception. What would that community look like to you?

**Take Action:** Consider making the spiritual disciplines part of your normal rhythm: daily, weekly, monthly, even yearly. Also, take the steps necessary to foster a community of people who practice these disciplines together. As a guide, consider using the *Spiritual Disciplines Handbook* by Adele Ahlberg Calhoun (InterVarsity Press, 2005).

THIS WEEK I WILL INCORPORATE THE FOLLOWING SPIRITUAL DISCIPLINE INTO MY DAILY LIFE: _____

**Pray:** Take a few moments to reflect on your answers to the questions and invite God into the ways you want to choose holiness as you commit to the practice of spiritual disciplines.

## GOING DEEPER (IF YOU WANT MORE)

**Read Hebrews 11.** This passage is often considered the "Hall of Faith." It's analogous to the Hall of Fame prevalent in most sports played around the world. In every Hall of Fame, at the collegiate or professional level, there are long lists of "greats"—people who have contributed to their sport in significant ways. The author of Hebrews, most presumably Paul, pauses here in Scripture to define *faith*, and to give us a long list of *faithful* "greats"—people who have chosen God's holiness over their personal freedom and commitment to God *in faith* above all else. And by doing so, they contributed to the foundations of Christianity and human history in significant ways, as listed in this passage. I would imagine that none of these individuals ever considered their story meaningful enough to include in the retelling of history. And yet there they are, and here we are today, reading about their faith in action. Here's what I want you to remember every time your mood changes and you go after your own personal freedoms: *fame is fleeting, but faith is eternal.* And faith in action is how we live out our commitment to holiness.

Spend extra time in prayer today as you consider how these individuals from the Hall of Faith made holiness—their pursuit of God—their number-one commitment in life. How do their faithful acts of holiness and commitment inspire the way you live your own life? Ask God to show you ways you can pursue holiness right where you are regardless of your circumstances.

**Use this space to jot down notes or thoughts as they come to mind.**

**For Next Week:** Review chapters four and nine in *Jesus Over Everything* and use the space below to write any insights or questions from your personal study that you want to discuss at the next group meeting. The teaching for session six, our last session, comes from chapter ten in *Jesus Over Everything*.

# WALKING IT ALL OUT

WE WILL SERVE THE LORD
OUR GOD AND OBEY HIM.

JOSHUA 24:24 NIV

# WELCOME

*Leader, read aloud to the group.*

Here's what is known to be true about the *Jesus-over-everything* journey: Remembering how good Jesus is to us is what compels us to put Jesus first. Jesus loves us—he loves *you*. When Jesus asks us to put him first, it's out of his great love for us. There will be days when putting Jesus over everything feels like a lot. But Jesus promises to do the heavy lifting. He's the only one who can sort out the hard, complicated mess of our lives and lighten our load, even as we take active steps to exalt him to his rightful place in our lives. Putting Jesus first won't always be easy, but it will *always* be worth it. My [Lisa's] own journey hasn't been easy; I have the bruises to show how hard I've fought to put *Jesus over everything,* and it's a daily discipline I have not perfected (nor will you).

At the end of the day, this study is all about the everyday choices of the Jesus-over-everything life. These choices are the disciplines and practices we've sown into our growth over the last five sessions together. If you've wanted to grow closer to Jesus, then the Jesus-overs (not to be confused with the deadly overs—their exact opposite) are the pathway: *real over pretty, honesty over hiding, service over spotlight, love over judgment, steady over hype, wisdom over knowledge, holiness over freedom,* and *commitment over moods.*

If you have read the book *Jesus Over Everything,* chapter 1, "The Land of the Deadly Overs," you'll recall further details of the place we often settle for that is full of cheap substitutes for fulfillment and hidden entrapments that promise us simplicity but, in the end, have led to complication. Conversely, Jesus over everything—a lifestyle, not a mantra—uncomplicates the complicated. This is the foundation on which to build the rest of our lives, not an addition to an existing structure. It is the agreement we make with God when we become followers of Jesus Christ. Jesus has the better "land" for us, but before we can take it, we must decide to put him in charge. It's his land to tend . . . his place to oversee. When Jesus is in first—the place he lived and died for—we find our truest identity and the most joyful, simple life. What more could we want?

# SHARE

*Briefly discuss one of the following statements:*

- Share one of your Take Action exercises from last week's between-sessions study. How has this made a difference for you as you put Jesus first?

— or —

- Name *one* area of your life where Jesus has been so good to you.

# READ

*Invite someone to read aloud the following passage as "heart prep" for Lisa's teaching. Listen for fresh insights as you hear the verses being read, and then briefly discuss the questions that follow.*

## JOSHUA INSTALLED AS LEADER

After the death of Moses the servant of the LORD, the LORD said to Joshua son of Nun, Moses' aide: "Moses my servant is dead. Now then, you and all these people, get ready to cross the Jordan River into the land I am about to give to them—to the Israelites. I will give you every place where you set your foot, as I promised Moses. Your territory will extend from the desert to Lebanon, and from the great river, the Euphrates—all the Hittite country—to the Mediterranean Sea in the west. No one will be able to stand against you all the days of your life. As I was with Moses, so I will be with you; I will never leave you nor forsake you. Be strong and courageous, because you will lead these people to inherit the land I swore to their ancestors to give them. Be strong and very courageous. Be careful to obey all the law my servant Moses gave you; do not turn from it to the right or to the left, that you may be successful wherever you go. Keep this Book of the Law always on your lips; meditate on it day and night, so that you may be careful to do everything written in it. Then you will be prosperous and successful. Have I not commanded you? Be strong and courageous. Do not be afraid; do not be discouraged, for the LORD your God will be with you wherever you go." (Joshua 1:1–9 NIV)

**What is one key insight that stands out to you from this passage?**

**Why do you think God repeats "be strong and courageous" so many times in conversation with Joshua?**

**As you listen to Lisa's teaching, consider where you need to hear "be strong and courageous" as you choose Jesus over everything,**

# WATCH

*Play the video segment for session six. As you watch, use the following outline to record any thoughts or concepts that stand out to you.*

## NOTES
### Real life

Ephesians 1—We need God as our compass

Malachi 4:2

YouTube video: *calves let out to pasture*

Freedom of sheer abandon

Fighting and pushing is not the way to feel free

*"When Jesus runs my life . . . my heart is free."*
Jesus over everything is a daily goal

## Go back to the basics

We crave simple because we're tired of so much information

God is good

God loves me

God cares

God sees

God knows

God has the whole world in his hands

Genesis 1—In the beginning . . .

The rest of the story: "on the seventh day, he rested"

*"Jesus has always been and will always be over everything."*

## Jesus is over EVERYTHING

The review of where we've been

Joshua 24:15

The land of the deadly overs—doing it our way

The land of Jesus-over-everything—doing it God's way

Take back possession of the promised land of our lives

**God created you. And Jesus is good no matter what.**

# DISCUSS

*Take a few minutes with your group members to discuss what you just watched and explore these concepts in Scripture.*

**1.** Name one word that describes your Jesus-over-everything journey since starting this study.

**2.** How has God provided direction or clarity for you over the previous sessions?

**3.** God delights in the joy and freedom we find in him, in our Jesus-over-everything life. Do you ever have the desire to run with sheer abandon like "calves let out to pasture"? What does this look like for you?

4. In what areas of your life have you begun to experience more freedom since putting Jesus first?

5. How have the spiritual disciplines you learned along the way contributed to living more of a simple, uncomplicated life?

6. Share one word to describe what it would feel like if you didn't have to be first in your life all the time.

# PRAY

*Pray as a group before you close your time together. Use this space to keep track of prayer requests and group updates.*

# FINAL PERSONAL STUDY

This is your last week of the *Jesus Over Everything* study. Let me encourage you to finish strong by doing all the exercises. Start with the reflection questions before moving on to the daily exercises. And if you haven't done so already, let me encourage you to read (or finish reading) *Jesus Over Everything*.

## WEEKLY REFLECTION: SESSION SIX

*Briefly review your video notes for session six. In the space below, write down the most significant point you took away from this session.*

Reflect on the word you chose at the end of the group session—the word that comes to mind when you think about not having to be first in your life anymore. List two or three *specific* ways that word will influence your decisions and actions this week as you put Jesus over everything else.

## DAY ONE: GOD'S PROMISES

Here's how I view this exercise. It's like sending one of my kids off to college, which I've now done twice. To the best of my ability, I want to make sure they're prepared for *every single thing* they're about to face, and I want them to know how much I love them. *Translation for this study:* I want you to be fully prepared to live the Jesus-over-everything life, and I want you to know how much I love you as you move forward in that beautiful endeavor. More importantly, I want you to know just how much God loves you. So. Stay with me, breathe in and exhale, and get ready for the grand finale. We're going to load up on a heavy dose of God's promises so that you are prepared to confidently put Jesus first over every single area in your life.

**Discover God's promises. Think about how God's promises uncomplicate your life as you fill in the chart below.**

| The Word | The Promise | How does this promise uncomplicate my life? |
| --- | --- | --- |
| Exodus 14:14 | | |
| Isaiah 40:31 | | |
| Isaiah 41:10 | | |
| Isaiah 54:10 | | |
| Jeremiah 29:11 | | |
| John 8:36 | | |
| James 1:5 | | |
| 1 John 1:9 | | |

I want you to see just how far you've come over these sessions with your choice to put Jesus over everything. Pick a few words that described your life prior to your journey to put Jesus first—your *before Jesus* words—and write those words in the left column. *Please know: These can be small progress and singular victories.* Then pick a few correlating words that describe the kind of life you want to live now—your *with Jesus* words—and write those in the center column. Finally, write a brief phrase describing how the shift from your "before Jesus" word to your "with Jesus" word has uncomplicated life for you.

| My life *before* Jesus over everything | My life *with* Jesus over everything | How this uncomplicates my life? |
| --- | --- | --- |
| | | |
| | | |
| | | |
| | | |
| | | |
| | | |
| | | |

Read Proverbs 3:1–8. If you grew up in the church, this will be a familiar passage. But don't skip over it just because you already know it. I want you to *really* read it. Read it slowly. Read it out loud, if that helps. And consider the following questions. According to this passage, what instructions are given on how to keep God's commandments and remember his promises? How does this bring "health to your body" and "nourishment to your bones"?

**Take Action:** Keeping God's commandments in your heart requires action. Maybe it's listening to God's Word while you exercise, or journaling God's promises during your quiet time. Maybe it's posting verses where you will see them most—such as the bathroom mirror—or memorizing passages of Scripture with your kids or coworkers. Whatever it is for you, I want you to figure out the best way to remember God's promises and keep God's commandments in your heart.

THIS WEEK I WILL REMEMBER GOD'S PROMISES BY:

_____

**Pray:** Take a few moments to reflect on your answers to the questions and invite God into the ways you want to keep his commandments and remember his promises.

## DAY TWO: THE PROMISED LAND

All this talk about the promised land can get a little confusing because if you're new to life with Jesus or new to the Bible, you may be asking, *"Which promised land is she talking about?"* But here's how I think God wants us to understand the promised land. The Israelites lived in the actual, physical promised land God had for them. There are historical records as well as Scripture to support this fact. But because of Jesus—his life, death, and resurrection—the new promised land for everyone who identifies as a follower of Jesus is life *with* him and *in* him. We get to live in the promised land of God when we put our faith and trust in Jesus Christ.

# COMMENTARY ON PROVERBS 3:1–8

These verses (up to verse 12) are probably a single unit of instruction. Here are the meanings of the key words and phrases used in these verses, as understood in the commentary of the *New Geneva Study Bible*:

**verse 1:** The Hebrew word for ["teaching" or] "law" is "torah," has the basic meaning of instruction and in Jewish tradition designates the Pentateuch. Wisdom's instruction, while not to be confused with the precepts of the Law of Moses, is likewise authoritative. The word "command" is also found in the law. As is typical of the parallel phrases of Hebrew poetry, the second half of the verse repeats the idea of the first half, clarifying it or expanding on it. Essentially, this verse means to memorize the commands and then put them into practice.

**verse 2:** The normal expectation is that wisdom will lead to a long, prosperous life, which is the blessing of God (Exodus 20:12). The word "peace" is the Hebrew term *shalom*. The term denotes general well-being, a harmony of relationships, wholeness and health (v. 8). In the Old Testament, the blessings of God are seen primarily in terms of this present life. It was not easy to reconcile this perspective with the suffering of the righteous or the prosperity of the wicked. The revelation that was to come with Christ and especially His resurrection from the dead was still far in the future.

**verse 3:** The Hebrew phrase [for] "mercy and truth" indicates clearly that wisdom is being advanced in a covenantal framework [some translations use the words "love and faithfulness"]. The instruction (v. 1) is practical teaching for life based on the character of God revealed in His Word. The metaphor of "bind them around your neck" indicates that wisdom will beautify one's life. And the metaphor of "write them on the tablet of your heart" is the same sense as v. 1. Make them a part of you by committing them to memory and then conforming your will to them.

**verse 5:** Rely entirely upon the Lord's Word and promises as revealed through the sage (Proverbs 2:6; 16:20). "Lean not on your own understanding" shows the contrast between the perception of reality that submits to God's revealed Word as the authority for all truth, and a perception that assumes human conjecture to have that authority.

**verse 6:** "Acknowledge Him" [or "submit to him"] is the practical expression of the mind that submits to God and knows Him. The Lord will guide you to the final goal of life. God gives wisdom and with it the task of making wise decisions; hint of guidance that bypasses the duty of making decisions. But human decisions do not overrule the protection of God's providence (Gen. 50:20, 21; Psalm 103:14).

**verse 7:** The phrase "wise in your own eyes" summarizes the idea that the human mind with its intellect and reason is independently capable of reaching a true understanding of reality, without any dependence upon God's revelation.

**verse 8:** True wisdom is life-affirming in the most practical ways.

–paraphrased from *New Geneva Study Bible*

- **Read:** Exodus 20:12. This is where the idea or expectation that wisdom leads to a long and prosperous life comes from; it's also God's blessing to us.
- **Look up:** Use a concordance to look up the term *blessing*. What other blessings are promised by God?
- **Explore:** How does wisdom show up in your life—in your actions, thoughts, prayers? In what ways have you received God's blessings in your life?

The Jesus-over everything-life is our "with God" lifestyle. It's our modern-day promised land. It's the place where God gives us peace and abundance, love and protection, joy and freedom. But it doesn't come without a cost. I have a dear friend who constantly reminds me that we have to be fierce about our promised land—about living our Jesus-over-everything life. We can't just "arrive" and assume the hard work is over. We have to be on the lookout for the thief who comes to steal, kill, and destroy

(John 10:10). Satan is always looking for opportunities to capture, snatch, ruin, or turn your promised land into desolate hopelessness. That's why you've got to anchor your life in the promises of God and claim that promised land with your whole heart.

But we're not the first ones on the verge of claiming our promised land. We have a lot to learn from the Israelites and their promised land journey. And we're also not the last ones, either. The way we lay claim to our promised land will influence the generations who come behind us. So let's lay hold of the land—the kind of life—God has promised us when we choose him over everything else.

**1.** Briefly review your reflections on God's promises from Day 1. How do the promises of God prepare you for moving into the promised land of God?

**2.** Using your own words, how would you describe the promised land that God has for you—your Jesus-over-everything life?

**3.** **Read Matthew 16:24–25.** According to this passage, what must we do to lay hold of our promised land?

**4.** **Read Genesis 12:7.** How did Abram respond when God showed him the promised land for his people? What would it look like for you to honor God in the same way today?

┌─ UNDERSTANDING YOUR BIBLE ─────────────────

# COMMENTARY ON MATTHEW 16:24–25

Then said Jesus unto his disciples . . . Knowing that they had all imbibed the same notion of a temporal kingdom, and were in expectation of worldly riches, honor, and pleasure; he took this opportunity of preaching the doctrine of the cross to them, and of letting them know, that they must prepare for persecutions, sufferings, and death; which they must expect to endure, as well as he, if they would be his disciples.

"If any man will come after me," that is, be a disciple and follower of him, it being usual for the master to go before, and the disciple to follow after him: now let it be who it will, rich or poor, learned or unlearned, young or old, male or female, that have any inclination and desire, or have took up a resolution in the strength of grace, to be a disciple of Christ,

let him deny himself: let him deny sinful self, ungodliness, and worldly lusts; and part with them, and his former sinful companions, which were as a part of himself: let him deny righteous self, and renounce all his own works of righteousness, in the business of justification and salvation; let him deny himself the pleasures and profits of this world, when in competition with Christ; let him drop and banish all his notions and expectations of an earthly kingdom, and worldly grandeur, and think of nothing but reproach, persecution, and death, for the sake of his Lord and Master: and

take up his cross; cheerfully receive, and patiently bear, every affliction and evil, however shameful and painful it may be, which is appointed for him, and he is called unto; which is his peculiar cross, as every Christian has his own; to which he should quietly submit, and carry, with an entire resignation to the will of God, in imitation of his Lord:

and follow me; in the exercise of grace, as humility, zeal, patience, and self-denial; and in the discharge of every duty, moral, or evangelical; and through sufferings and death, to his kingdom and glory. The allusion is, to Christ's bearing his own cross, and Simeon's carrying it after him, which afterwards came to pass.

*—Gill's Exposition of the Entire Bible*

- **Read:** Mark 8:34–38. This is Mark's translation of the words of Jesus.
- **Look up:** Use a concordance to look up the term *cross*. Notice how, where, and when this term is used.
- **Explore:** What do you think Jesus means when he says, *"take up your cross"*? What does it mean for *you* to take up your cross?

5. **Read Joshua 5:6.** Like the Israelites who walked in the wilderness for forty years, sometimes we catch a glimpse of the promised land—our Jesus-over-everything life—but we're delayed in moving into it because we haven't cleared out the sin required to enter. Is there anything holding you back from putting Jesus first in all areas of your life? What sin do you need to confess so that you can enter in?

6. The promised land isn't just a carrot God dangles on a stick, hoping we make good choices; it's a *covenant* between God and his people—us. It's a *promise* regarding the *promised land*. That's why as the Israelites are about to cross over into the land, they are reminded *three* times of God's promise, *"I will never leave you nor forsake you"* (Deuteronomy 31:6, 8; Joshua 1:5). And God does the same with us. Because of Jesus, we have the presence of the Holy Spirit who will never leave us or forsake us. How does God's promise to never leave you nor forsake you give you the courage to live the Jesus-over-everything life?

**Take Action:** Today I want you to pause and reflect on what this idea of living in the promised land means for you. And I want you to embrace God's desire for you to live in the promised land—your Jesus-over-everything lifestyle—by trusting God with the complicated mess of your life and resting in the exchange he's making daily to uncomplicate your life.

In what ways might you embrace the goodness of God today? Is it to pause and notice the way God is loving you? Is it to express your gratitude to God in prayer, journaling, or song? Is it to actually allow yourself to experience the joy and delight of God's goodness by celebrating with something fun? Is it to rest—actually take a rest or a nap—in God's promises? A wise spiritual mentor once told me the most holy thing we could do sometimes was to sleep, and I've carried that good word with me ever since. Whatever you sense God encouraging you to do in this moment in response to his goodness and his invitation to life in the promised land, do it.

I WILL EMBRACE LIFE IN THE PROMISED LAND OF GOD BY:

_____

**Pray:** Take a few moments to reflect on the idea that you get to live in the promised land of God when you place Jesus over everything. Express your gratitude to God for his constant presence in your life.

## DAY THREE: WALKING IT ALL OUT

If you were to read the entire book of Joshua (I highly recommend it), then you would read about the Israelites and their journey into the promised land. There we see that *arriving* in the promised land wasn't enough; they actually had to take *possession* of the land and claim it as their own. The first half of the book of Joshua includes stories many of us have heard before—Rahab and the spies, Joshua and the battle of Jericho, the drying up of the Jordan River, the sun standing still, and the allotment of land for all twelve tribes of Israel. And then we get halfway through the book of Joshua, where we see that there are tribes still waiting to take possession of their land. And Joshua says, *"How long will you wait before you begin to take possession of the land that the Lord, the God of your ancestors, has given you?"* (Joshua 18:3 NIV). I imagine he said this with an impatient tone like a frustrated parent, like *"Come on everybody, what are you waiting for?!"*

┌─────────────────────────────────────────────────────────────┐

UNDERSTANDING YOUR BIBLE

# WHAT DOES THE PHRASE "TO TAKE POSSESSION" MEAN?

In the original Hebrew of the Old Testament, *to take possession* means: inherit, dispossess; to occupy, consume, driving out, enjoy, expel, to seize.

יָרַשׁ / yarash or yaresh

This word and various forms of this word appear in Hebrew 231 times throughout the Old Testament.

—from Strong's Hebrew 3423 and *Strong's Exhaustive Concordance*

- **Read:** Also read Judges 2:6–23. This passage highlights what happened to the Israelites as a result of their disobedience to God. At some point, they stopped possessing the promised land in the way they were commanded to do so and quickly turned from the ways of their ancestors.
- **Look up:** Look up *possess* in a concordance to learn about more examples of *inheritance* and *taking possession* throughout Scripture.
- **Explore:** Consider what it means for you to fully possess—lay claim on—your faith. If God has cleared the way for you to inherit his blessings—this can be something tangible or intangible—consider what's holding you back from fully embracing those blessings.

└─────────────────────────────────────────────────────────────┘

God has every right to get frustrated with me in so many cases, and I suspect, you too. Some of us are standing at the edge of the promised land on this Jesus-first journey, and we still haven't claimed our land. Some of us have come so far and are so very close to laying claim on the life God has created us to live—the uncomplicated, simple life of Jesus first. I don't want to push you into the land or twist your arm. I want you to lay claim on that land because you know it's best for you. All of us have to come to this realization on our own, with the Holy Spirit's prompting. I'm praying and trusting this study has been a catalyst in that process for you. But it's God's work, not mine. My great desire is for us to cross that finish line together today into the *Jesus-over-everything* life, as we reflect on what it looks like to walk it all out.

**1.** How would you describe where you are today: you've laid claim of your promised land—your Jesus-over-everything life, *or* you're still standing at the edge thinking about it? Why?

**2.** Whether you've already laid claim to your Jesus-over-everything life or you're about to do that today, what fears or challenges do you have about walking it all out?

**3.** How have you already experienced the joy of a Jesus-first life? How has Jesus already uncomplicated life for you since you started walking out your new journey? What are you most looking forward to in your life with Jesus over everything, both short-term and long-term?

**4. Read Joshua 21:43–45.** What happened once *all* the Israelite tribes took possession of their land? How has God given you peace and rest in your journey too?

**5.** **Read Joshua 23:14.** What reminder does Joshua leave with the Israelites before he says farewell and passes away? How does this reminder encourage your heart too?

**6.** **Read 2 Corinthians 1:20–22.** What does this passage say about God's promises? How has God laid claim on our lives? What hope does this leave you with?

**Take Action:** Mark this moment—the moment you realized the promised land is for you too, as you choose Jesus over everything. I told you about my shopping overindulgence earlier in this study. And while I want you to be mindful of consumerism as a substitute for putting Jesus first, I also want to encourage you with a little freedom here. I have a friend who likes to pick up small mementos to mark her spiritual journey and major accomplishments in life. She will often do this for close friends too. To date, she has a few river rocks she's collected over the years as well as a small pair of earrings and a hammered bracelet—all reminders of the work God has been doing in her life.

Look for something this week that reminds you that you have decided to lay claim and take possession of your promised land, and you are now walking out the Jesus-over-everything life. It could be a small memento or piece of jewelry, as my friend collects, or something you already have in your home—a picture of nature, a piece of artwork, or a note you wrote to yourself during this study. Then go the extra mile to find a creative way to remind a fellow friend and Jesus-follower that she too is walking it all out in the promised land of God.

I WILL REMIND MYSELF AND MY FRIEND THAT WE LIVE IN THE PROMISED LAND OF GOD BY: _____

**Pray:** Take a few moments to reflect on the idea that you get to take hold of the promised land of God when you put Jesus over everything; express your gratitude to God for this remarkable gift.

## GOING DEEPER (IF YOU WANT MORE)

**Read Ephesians 1.** Have you ever stopped to consider the idea that God also has a promised land—and it is in our hearts? Our hearts are the place of God's possession when we live the *Jesus-over-everything* life. That's why I love this passage so much, because it reminds us that *we* are God's possession—we are the *praise of his glory* (Ephesians 1:14 NIV).

Spend extra time in prayer today as you consider the promised land God has for you as a result of placing Jesus first in your life. And reflect on the idea that you and your heart are God's promised land and his reason for praise.

**Use this space to jot down notes or thoughts as they come to mind.**

# EPILOGUE

Huge hugs and high fives . . . we did it, my friend. This has been a sweet Jesus-over-everything journey together. But the journey doesn't end here. This is the kind of journey you will travel every single day for the rest of your life as you choose time and again to put Jesus first. There will be hard days and days you are less successful, and initially, it may feel mostly uphill. But like with every practice, it will become more natural and, I pray over time, something you learn to love and live. There's no way around it: Jesus first *is* the way to the simpler life. Our impulse to run *from* Jesus because of sin and shame will eventually turn into a tendency to run *to* Jesus for reprieve from the complication, difficulty, and pain. The more we practice putting Jesus in first place, the more we do it out of healthy habit.

If you're struggling, please don't lose hope. Whether you're staring at the promised land, still deciding if you want to take possession, *or* struggling with the daily discipline to choose Jesus over everything time and time again, *God is with you.* He will never leave you nor forsake you, and *all* his promises are true.

Besides, your new beautiful reality is that now you have a community of friends who are on this journey with you. Lean on one another, encourage one another, challenge one another, and pray for one another. God never intended for us to live our wild, wonderful, holy lives alone. He created us in relationship with him *for* relationship with each other. If you're feeling hopeless, please share those feelings with Jesus, and then, if you feel so led, share them with a trusted friend. Get some sleep. And then start fresh with Jesus again tomorrow. Remember: until we go to heaven, this earthly Jesus-over-everything journey is daily and ongoing.

If you're doing well today, praise Jesus. Keep going. We never mature past a daily need for confession, repentance, and checking ourselves to make sure Jesus is at the top of the list.

And always know: Jesus stays ready and willing to uncomplicate our lives. If we will give him the priority he deserves, he will reorder our lives back to a place of simplicity. It is a choice for the very best life.

I love you. I love him most. Truly, he is everything.

*Lisa*

Now to him who is able to do immeasurably more than all
we ask or imagine, according to his power that is at work
within us, to him be glory in the church and in Christ Jesus
throughout all generations, for ever and ever! Amen.

—EPHESIANS 3:20 NIV

# LEADER'S GUIDE

Thank you for your willingness to lead your group through this study! What you have chosen to do is valuable and will make a great difference in the lives of others. The rewards of being a leader are different from those of participating, and we hope that as you lead you will find your own walk with Jesus deepened by this experience.

*Jesus Over Everything* is a six-session study built around video content and small-group interaction. As the group leader, just think of yourself as the host of a dinner party. Your job is to take care of your guests by managing all the behind-the-scenes details so that when everyone arrives, they can just enjoy time together.

As the group leader, your role is not to answer all the questions or reteach the content—the video, book, and study guide will do most of that work. Your job is to guide the experience and cultivate your small group into a kind of teaching community. This will make it a place for members to process, question, and reflect—not receive more instruction.

Before your first meeting, make sure everyone in the group gets a copy of the study guide. This will keep everyone on the same page and help the process run more smoothly. If some group members are unable to purchase the guide, arrange it so that people can share the resource with other group members. Giving everyone access to all the material will position this study to be as rewarding an experience as possible. Everyone should feel free to write in his or her study guide and bring it to group every week.

Every member of your group now has full access to watch videos from the convenience of their chosen devices at any time—for missed group meetings, for rewatching, for sharing teaching with others, or watching videos individually and then meeting if your group is short on meeting time and that makes the group experience doable and more realistic. Be sure to login and do a test run of following the streaming access instructions (found on the inside front cover) so you can easily talk your group through their own access set up.

If you have questions or struggle at any point, please contact customer service at 800-727-3480.

## SETTING UP THE GROUP

You will need to determine with your group how long you want to meet each week so you can plan your time accordingly. Generally, most groups like to meet for either ninety minutes or two hours, so you could use one of the following schedules:

| Section | 90 Minutes | 120 Minutes |
|---|---|---|
| **Welcome** (members arrive and get settled) | 10 minutes | 15 minutes |
| **Share** (discuss one or more of the opening questions for the session) | 10 minutes | 15 minutes |
| **Read** (discuss the questions based on the Scripture reading for the week) | 10 minutes | 15 minutes |
| **Watch** (watch the teaching material together and take notes) | 20 minutes | 20 minutes |
| **Discuss** (discuss the Bible study questions you selected ahead of time) | 30 minutes | 40 minutes |
| **Respond / Pray** (pray together as a group and dismiss) | 10 minutes | 15 minutes |

As the group leader, you'll want to create an environment that encourages sharing and learning. A church sanctuary or formal classroom may not be as ideal as a living room, because those locations can feel formal and less intimate. No matter what setting you choose, provide enough comfortable seating for everyone, and, if possible, arrange the seats in a semicircle so everyone can see the video easily. This will make transition between the video and group conversation more efficient and natural.

Also, try to get to the meeting site early so you can greet participants as they arrive. Simple refreshments create a welcoming atmosphere and can be a wonderful addition to a group study evening. Try to take food and pet allergies into account to make your guests as comfortable as possible. You may also want to consider offering childcare to couples with children who want to attend. Finally, be sure your media technology is working properly. Managing these details up front will make the rest of your group experience flow smoothly and provide a welcoming space in which to engage the content of *Jesus Over Everything*.

## STARTING THE GROUP TIME

Once everyone has arrived, it's time to begin the group. Here are some simple tips to make your group time healthy, enjoyable, and effective.

First, begin the meeting with a short prayer and remind the group members to put their phones on silent. This is a way to make sure you can all be present with one another and with God. Next, give each person a few minutes to respond to the questions in the "Share" and "Read" sections. This won't require as much time in session one, but beginning in session two, people will need more time to share their insights from their personal studies. Usually, you won't answer the discussion questions yourself, but you should go first with the "Share" and "Read" questions, answering briefly and with a reasonable amount of transparency.

At the end of session one, invite the group members to complete the between-sessions personal studies for that week. Explain that you will be providing some time before the video teaching next week for anyone to share insights. Let them know sharing is optional, and it's no problem if they can't get to some of the between-sessions activities some weeks. It will still be beneficial for them to hear from the other participants and learn about what they discovered.

# LEADING THE DISCUSSION TIME

Now that the group is engaged, it's time to watch the video and respond with some directed small-group discussion. Encourage all the group members to participate in the discussion, but make sure they know they don't have to do so. As the discussion progresses, you may want to follow up with comments such as, "Tell me more about that," or, "Why did you answer that way?" This will allow the group participants to deepen their reflections and invite meaningful sharing in a nonthreatening way.

Note that you have been given multiple questions to use in each session, and you do not have to use them all or even follow them in order. Feel free to pick and choose questions based on either the needs of your group or how the conversation is flowing. Also, don't be afraid of silence. Offering a question and allowing up to thirty seconds of silence is okay. It allows people space to think about how they want to respond and also gives them time to do so.

As group leader, you are the boundary keeper for your group. Do not let anyone (yourself included) dominate the group time. Keep an eye out for group members who might be tempted to "attack" folks they disagree with or try to "fix" those having struggles. These kinds of behaviors can derail a group's momentum, so they need to be steered in a different direction. Model active listening and encourage everyone in your group to do the same. This will make your group time a safe space and create a positive community.

The group discussion leads to a closing time of individual reflection and prayer. Encourage the participants to take a few moments to review what they've learned during the session and write down their thoughts to the "Respond" section. This will help them cement the big ideas in their minds as you close the session. Conclude by having the participants break into smaller groups of two to three people to pray for one another.

Thank you again for taking the time to lead your group. You are making a difference in the lives of others and having an impact on the kingdom of God!

# BIBLE STUDY
# SOURCE
## —for women—
powered by ChurchSource

Connecting you with hundreds of
# WOMEN'S BIBLE STUDIES
## FROM YOUR FAVORITE BIBLE TEACHERS

| LISA WHITTLE | LYSA TERKEURST | ANNE GRAHAM LOTZ | JESS CONNOLLY | REBEKAH LYONS |

Providing
# WOMEN'S MINISTRY AND
# SMALL GROUP LEADERS

with the **INSPIRATION, ENCOURAGEMENT, AND RESOURCES** to grow your ministry